The Production of Society

The Production of Society

*A Marxian Foundation
for Social Theory*

Michael E. Brown

*Queens College and The Graduate School of
The City University of New York*

Rowman & Littlefield
PUBLISHERS

ROWMAN & LITTLEFIELD

Published in the United States of America in 1986
by Rowman & Littlefield, Publishers
(a division of Littlefield, Adams & Company)
81 Adams Drive, Totowa, New Jersey 07512

Copyright © 1986 by Rowman & Littlefield

Library of Congress Cataloging-in-Publication Data

Brown, Michael E.
  The production of society.

  Bibliography: p. 147
  Includes index.
  1. Communism and society   2. Marxian school of
sociology.   I. Title.
HX542.B717   1986   335.4′1   86-6424
ISBN 0-8476-7472-X
ISBN 0-8476-7473-8 (pbk.)

88 87 86
10 9 8 7 6 5 4 3 2 1

Printed in the United States of America

Contents

Preface

THE MOVE AWAY from Marx's "labor theory of value" has proceeded at an increasing pace for over a decade and a half. It represents,
in large part, a response to economists' criticisms that the theory fails
to account for the vicissitudes of the price-making money market,
which is, in turn, the result of an over-emphasis on labor theory in the
first volume of Marx's major work, *Capital,* and on essentially illustrative materials in the second and third volumes.

There are, of course, other cogent reasons for this: the incompleteness of *Capital* raises legitimate questions about Marx's own understanding of what would constitute a full critique of capital; the way in
which Marx set about to measure value was ambiguous as to whether
he intended to define value by labor time or by a concept still to be
clarified; some parts of the Marxian tradition in research suggest a type
of scientific methodology whose standards seem either inconsistent
with the Marxian metatheory or are too rigorous for what can legitimately be done with it; the possibility has been raised that exploitation
and social conflict can be understood without taking recourse to
something so ill-defined or difficult to apply as the concept of value;
finally, it has been argued, and this seems to be the strongest extra-
economic position, that the Marxian theory of value expressed in
Volume 1 of *Capital* is adequate only for the analysis of relatively
simple capitalist economies and therefore appropriate, if at all, only for
a nineteenth century reality (cf. the "Value Symposium" in *Science &
Society,* Winter, 1984–1985, and David Gleicher's comment on the
symposium, 1985–1986).

But if the theory of value expressed in Volume 1 is only a first
approximation, requiring a refinement possible only through the extended analyses of Volumes 2 and 3, incomplete and ambiguous though
they are, and if the interpretation of "value" depends upon what Marx
could have meant by his transformation of "class" to "the society of
the producers," it may be possible to recover what value theory
contributes to social science, regardless of the criticisms that have
been made of it. On the other hand, if Marx meant to develop, as I

believe he did, a sociology, it must be something quite different from the field as presently defined.

The fact that this book emphasizes the connections of Marxian theory to psychoanalysis and ethnomethodology, and not merely in the form of synthesis, suggests a direction such a sociology might follow. In order to establish that direction, however, I have found it necessary 1. to stay within the confines of the critique of capital, 2. to speculate beyond the formal limits of the theory in ways that may occasionally seem extravagant but that are necessary to an appreciation of what is implicit in the sociological version of that critique, 3. to make the theory explicit without the sort of critical review of debates within the field that is usually expected of such a text, and 4. to cite references (other than those to Marx's writings) as generally relevant to the argument rather than as specific scholarly resources from which the argument was drawn. In a sense, then, this book is an exercise in metasociology intended to provide a Marxian foundation for sociology and a sociological foundation for the social sciences, or at least a prologue to foundations. Above all, it provides an interpretation of Marx's critique of capital for which "the society of the producers" is realized discursively as well as politically, organizationally, and as part of the complex and contradictory relation of production and circulation. Therefore, it contains something of a theory of praxis and interprets that in regard to the ethnomethodological studies of Harold Garfinkel.

In this book I attempt to make a prima facie case for the use of the labor theory of value as a metasociology for the following reasons: 1. the labor theory in its extended expression provides a view of society as historically dynamic in the sense that social change is constant and immanent; 2. it establishes, through the part it plays in the critique of capital, connections among local actions and between them and the ensemble of social relations that determine their conditions; 3. its emphasis on the unrepeatability of social process restores the historical dimension to the critique of capital from which it had been all but eliminated by post-Althusserian hyperstructural models of the capitalist mode of production; 4. it formulates connections between the productive activities of people and the social relations that make those activities productive; 5. it relies on and validates a self-critical methodology that is consistent with two fundamental ideas about the proper subject matter of social science—the internal relation of theory to practice and the immanence of self-consciousness (or self-reflection) to all things that can be taken as humanly social; 6. it is an organizing principle for an enormous wealth of literature that is only now being interpreted and debated as an interdisciplinary field of study.

The overemphasis on Volume 1 of *Capital,* and economistic interpretations of the second and third volumes based on that overemphasis, has led to a rejection of the core of Marxian theory that is entirely sectoral, to economics strictly defined, but that has flowed over into the other social sciences without, I believe, an adequate extraeconomic evaluation of the grounds for that rejection. Even proponents have chosen to argue the point along strictly economic lines. While this debate is not irrelevant to the politics of the socialist movement, and in any case has helped to clarify problems that Marx's work left untouched or undeveloped, it has been entirely too restrictive of the theoretical problem of evaluating the significance of Marxism for social science. The relation of base and superstructure has borne most of the criticism in this area. It has led, in the context of the rejection of the labor theory of value, to an emphasis on culture both as an area of research for reformulating a "critical" social science and an alternative "base" for a new dialectic of consensus and polity.

While I do not wish directly to engage in those debates, this book is relevant to the question of how much weight they ought to be given in discussions of the significance of Marxian theory for modern social thought. Essentially, I argue that society must be conceived of in historical terms, where 1. "historical terms" refers to the dynamics of an activity (taken locally or globally) rather than to successions of events or causes and effects; 2. the possibility of identifying the historical features of capitalism rests on the validity of the theory of value; 3. the validity of the theory of value depends upon an interpretation of it in regard to Marx's discussion of "the society of the producers" and the reformulations of "class," "exploitation," and the contradictions of production and circulation that occur in Volume 3 of *Capital;* 4. the interpretation of value in regard to "the society of the producers" is reasonable both in the terms enunciated in Volumes 2 and 3 and in the appendix to Volume 1 (1976), and because of Marx's insistence on the status of Volume 1 as an "abstraction."

If this interpretation is valid and useful, then Marx can be said to have written a foundation for an authentically sociological theory that does not fall under the criticisms leveled at an interpretation of his work as economics or even, in the strict sense, political economy. It follows that the theory of value is not intended to address the problems of inequality, the exploitation of one group by another, the vicissitudes of price, or the local determinations of rationally organized productive activity. It is instead an analysis of the relationship between locally organized activities and the ensemble of affairs on which they depend and with which they are in one way or another interdependent. The emphasis on production per se, in Volume 1, becomes an emphasis on the society that produces itself, and so, establishes a sociology of process rather than of structure, history rather than purposes and products, self-reflection rather than impulse.

I begin by situating Marxian thought and proceed through a discussion of the labor theory of value and its relationship to a variety of sociological topics. Discussions of the latter are not intended to be exhaustive but, for the most part, illustrative. The final sections link my interpretation of Marxian theory to versions of discourse analysis and the contemporary sense of subject-object dialectic that it constitutes. The book makes no pretense at being directly relevant to politically strategic considerations as such, though it is intended to be indirectly so. It is, if it succeeds, an intervention in a literature that has seen many interventions. Currently, a number of important compilations have been published that attempt to reassess the impact of Marxism on the social sciences and that of contemporary social science on Marxian thought (cf., for example, Anderson 1976, 1983; Ollman and Vernoff 1982, 1984; Bottomore, et al. 1983; Wolff and Resnick 1985; the comprehensive formulations of Marxian theory by Poulantzas 1975a, 1975b, 1978; and the Marxian and socialist journals that have so conscientiously sustained a high level of discussion over the years, especially *Socialist Review, Telos, New Left Review, Monthly Review, KapitaliState, Social Text, Radical America, Science & Society,* and the *Journal of Radical Political Economy.*

The Production of Society

1

Marx and Marxism

Until the end of the eighteenth century, the ideas of nation and society served ideological rather than speculative purposes. Their connections in learned discourse were matters of convenience rather than discipline. Taken together, the terms evoked a sense of common experience that could only be shared by those whose property rested on a militarily defensible national state. It is no wonder, then, that their use served more to mobilize sentiment among the gentry than to formulate the practical limits of state policy and the theoretical limits of the idea of nationalism on which that policy increasingly depended.

It was ultimately impossible, however, to ignore the implications of diplomacy in international affairs and bureacracy in the affairs of the domestic polity. The fact that force was a component in both the consolidation of the nation and the maintenance of internal order could no longer satisfy the theoretical need to formulate an idea of society adequate to the complex situation of alienable property, centralized decision, and mobile and increasingly agglomerated populations. Problems of compliance and cooperation, rationalization and communication, had to be addressed as people accumulated in towns and cities, local traditions were over-thrown, and vast orders of production were begun at sites of what would eventually be called modern industry.

As a result, and in the context of the enormous success of the mercantile interest, it was only a matter of time before political economy acquired the paradigmatic and technical aspects of a disciplined science. Adam Smith brought the concepts of society and nation together under the auspices of an overwhelming awareness of the social significance of economy: "society" was qualified by its most salient fact, commerce, while "nation" summarized the practical confluence of considerations of boundary and wealth in an epoch in which policy was king.

Despite his optimism, *The Wealth of Nations* captured the bleak aspect of the progress of commerce by recognizing an inevitable separation of social condition from individual effort. At the margin of commercial society, competition within the price-making market would prove statistically unfavorable to a definite few. This liability to impoverishment would pose one of the main qualifications of the *laissez-faire* principle of commerce's proper governance. The fact that this outcome required governmental policy primarily aimed at managing the most general features of the national economy rather than at controlling economic activities taken singly made it seem that state involvement in economic affairs would never reach a point of even detectable excess. The fact that market-induced poverty depended on bad luck, as well as on the weaknesses of the victims or their lack of personal enterprise, placed it outside the harsher strictures of commercial morality.

Poverty that reflected general social conditions rather than the specifics of character, however, posed an important question for classical economics: what is it about the relationship between commerce and wealth on a national scale that bodes ill for some people regardless of their shrewdness, courage, diligence, or adherance to the Protestant work ethic? This would eventually raise a deeper question about the relationship of price and value; but for the classical economists it placed systematic economics above the individually oriented "science" of thrift, and at the same time complicated the Malthusian idea of natural scarcity by introducing elements of a socio-historical explanation. Eventually, monopoly and poverty would take their places among the most important problems addressed in debates over the role of the state in modern society.

Clearly, if only implicitly, Smith taught that commerce alone could not provide universal freedom or a foundation for a totally rational economic policy. The reconciliation of *labor,* what Marx would finally refer to as "the society of the producers," and *profits,* the ordering of material life by the market, was presaged in *The Wealth of Nations* as the problematic for the next development in economic thought. Because it was a period of transition, however, the eighteenth century could provide no clear articulation of the class relations of what would eventually become recognizable as an historically specific mode of production, that of capital. Therefore, Smith was unable to gauge the societal ramifications of the historically decisive problem identified by his work.

"Commercial society" finally gave way to "capitalism," and to the material and discursive practices that would, from the middle of the nineteenth century, give direction and interdisciplinary latitude to political economy. From that point, history would have its material dimension so crucial to later theories of "evolution," political science, its relation to problems of constituencies and distribution; and sociology, its relation to the practical entanglements of "value" (cf. Small

1972). By midcentury, the academy had to acknowledge in theory what sections of the new industrial working class had already discovered in the practice of political mobilization across the normally divisive lines of craft, income, region, and traditions: "free enterprise" was free only for the few whose privileges depended unequivocally on a new kind of bondage for the many. Chartism had given the class dimension to politics and the political dimension to the struggles of a growing proletariat. Underscoring the more vivid displays of this conflict were reports of the "statisticians" and factory inspectors that showed, with unmistakable clarity and drama, that labor's expense in the "freely entered" wage contract included hardship, merciless employment, and social degradation.

Thus, before Karl Marx had put pen to paper, the inequities of capitalism were apparent and familiar. What were not obvious was the constitutive role these inequities played in a mode of production geared to the private accumulation of wealth, and the dependence of the economy of capital on a steadily expanding socialization of labor that it could neither rationalize nor maintain. Marx clarified these insights in terms of the sociohistorical implications of the Hegelian dialectic, and by establishing his analysis on the discursive terrain occupied by the classical economists and their descendants. The former emphasized the contradictory aspects of the material/civil order and their implications for general social development. The latter gave Marx the language with which to raise the prevailing intuition about the problematic relations of labor and capital to the level of a rigorous critical analysis of the capitalist mode of production. His theory reached its climactic formulation in the transformation of the idea of "wealth" as "the wealth of nations" to that of "the wealth of society." In this respect it established the foundation for a theory of society and, in that regard, demonstrated the significance of the "political" in "political economy" to the struggle of social classes over the constitution and disposition of social wealth.

In this respect too, Marx's theory articulated a modern secular morality in terms of historically appropriate conceptions of social interest (class), universal value (the end of exploitation), collectivity (cooperation in the production of social wealth), and practical reason (the critical reproduction of cooperation), and provided a philosophically plausible conception of democracy (the social control of the means of reproducing society) free of the evolutionary individualism of bourgeois civil society and the corporatist liberalism of hegemonic capital.

His analysis led him to criticize various proposals offered by his contemporaries in response to two obvious paradoxes of western industrialization: 1. the coexistence of a rapidly expanding productive capacity and increasing poverty; 2. the social chaos brought about by the steady concentration and fiscal rationalization of capital.

He rejected a temptation, popular even today, to address the first paradox by advocating reforms that would be initiated singly and without further guarantee either by the state or through negotiations between those at the base of society and those holding effective power. It was apparent that operational reforms offered by those whose practices were to be the object of reform were compromised at the outset. Moreover, to the extent that the available means for implementing reforms were already constrained by those practices, their use could only be consistent with and contribute to their founding interests. Regardless of those defects, the parameters of negotiation were too well established within an unyielding context of inequality to take the results of negotiation for granted. Even gains achieved by legal and parliamentary means had to be protected by a still more radical politics in order to avoid reinforcing precisely the conditions they were intended to ameliorate.

Marx rejected as well the temptation to redress the second paradox by utopian appeals to the virtues of the past. This nostalgic option was unacceptable for several reasons: 1. "pre-capitalist" life was, contrary to utopian myth, harsh in the scarcities it took for granted and brutal in the powers required to apportion them. The feudal economy and the local economies of the farmer and craftsman lacked the coordination necessary to nourish precisely those modern masses whose lamentable condition would presumably justify the return to earlier orders of subsistence production and local tradition. 2. history is not merely the passage of time but the coordination and practical transcendence of human effort. Therefore, it can not be reversed without destroying the society that the utopian return to the past was intended to save. Marx had no doubt that capitalism provided new means for domesticating nature and appropriating its fruits to the needs of a global economy. But the human cost of its limited success was exploitation, oppression, and misery on a hitherto unprecedented scale. While it was essential, as reformists and utopians vaguely understood, to complete the capitalist revolution of production by eliminating the "war of all against all" that continually undermined it, any movement backwards could only reinstate the conditions of scarcity, brutality, and stultifying traditions that capitalism responded to in the first place.

Criticisms of the burdens imposed by industry and commerce on their populations were abundantly in evidence throughout the nineteenth century. Marx, however, showed that these burdens were the result of an inequality of classes that was both unavoidable in capitalist production and represented in all its products. The decisive point was that the source of inequality lay in exploitive relations of production that were incompatible with the cooperative activity on which economic expansion depended. Marx's conclusion was practically as well as theoretically important, for the economically creative element of society was its socialized labor force: capitalism depended upon the coordinated energies expended by its workers organized in production as a class, yet it could not sustain the social conditions of that class's productivity.

The justification and extension of this idea has come to be known as "Marxism." Marx's own writings were the first systematic account of the political, social, and economic dimensions of capitalism. The Marxian tradition consists of well over a century of writing and research in countless languages. Its major works explore the historical and sociological significance of several controversial theses: 1. the capitalist economy is regulated, if at all, by its organization of production rather than by its market and the ostensible rationality of self-interested exhange; 2. capitalist production depends upon contradictory rather than systematic relations of production; 3. all aspects of capitalist society reflect in one way of another the centrality and contradictory character of the capitalist mode of production. None of these theses implies causal determinism. None implies that all that people do can be subsumed by the concept "capitalist society." The form of determination implicit in Marxian theory and the limits of the Marxian conception of "society" will be discussed in the chapters to follow.

Much of what we currently think of as sociology, economics, and political science can be seen as attempts either to refute these theses, to use them to organize research and analysis, or to qualify them for application to sectoral studies. Marxian thought is one of the central intellectual resources of Western scholarship and one of the major sources of democratic theory and secular ethics. Its importance to social science lies 1. in the fact that it is the only theoretical tradition that examines the relationship between the limited, and volatile, unity of capitalism and its history; and 2. in the fact that it is the only discipline that has formulated a concept of "society" consistent with a conception of "history" as the self-reflecting course of human interaction and accomplishment.

2

An Introduction to the Sociology of Capitalism

$\mathcal{J}$ AT ITS MOST GENERAL, Marxian theory accounts for how capitalism works and how it changes. Its distinctive foci are history and economy. Its theoretical power lies in its identification and analysis of those problems for which capitalism has been a solution (such as underproduction) and those which capitalist economy cannot solve without undergoing profound social transformation.

It is necessary at the outset to distinguish between the history of a *society* and what happens to *a people* or *a territory*. Marxian theory defines "history" as the internal transformation of socioeconomic relations, a dynamic or problem-related and self-oriented process that involves the most universal aspects of a society. External forces that impinge upon a people or territory may establish conditions that limit the internal processes of social transformation, or place limitations upon them; but the two are theoretically distinct. The fact that geopolitics has recognized as juridical elements nations and nationalities rather than social and material interdependencies often confuses the issue. The history of nations is the record of territory, rule, and war; that of societies is the self-transformation of social relations. For the first, boundaries are claims prior to action; for the second, they are representations of events. The identification of *society* as independent of *nation* is a fundamental rule of analysis. It is predicated upon a critique of the classical view that "civil society" is a natural formation evolving in part from conditions of settlement; but in any case it is a necessary feature of any historical sociology that attempts to comprehend the processes that underlie the appearance of structure.

NATION AND SOCIETY

One often speaks of a nation as if it were a society. But the former is merely a putative unity of enforced recognition, while the latter is a unity of practice established by social relations of mutual interdependence. A nation may be sustained by force, tradition, agreement, or apathy, but it cannot sustain itself. It may be ruled, but it has no history, no dynamic aspect besides the limited history of its ruling agency or the occasionally accidental confluence of social relations and territory.[1] A society, on the other hand, is an inclusive ordering of human affairs in which the most general relations among people must be enacted self-consciously if those affairs are to have order. In other words, and with qualifications yet to be discussed, a nation may be ordered, but a society orders itself.

The most inclusive ordering of human affairs that can presently be admitted as social is the coordination, regardless of territory, of the material conditions of collective action. This is why Marxian theory characterizes society as a problematic unity of practice established by social relations of production (in the sense of an interaction of mutually relevant activities considered from the standpoint of the reliability of the unity they make possible) and, as such, an historically specific formation. This unity may be influenced by and dependent upon the external fact of national recognition, and compromised by the cultural incorporation of that fact, but it is essential to the Marxian theoretical enterprise that society be understood as an analytically independent object.

PRACTICE AND STRUCTURE

The practice of this unity is a dialectic of collective action and reflection, an interpenetration of what people do together and what their collectivity makes of whatever they have done. "Dialectic" refers to the constant movement back and forth from activity to reflection, each moment of which depends upon changes that have taken place at one or the other pole. What collectivities make of what they have done depends upon, but does not replicate or in any other way directly reproduce, what they have made of what they did before.

The term "practice" is used when there is emphasis on the movement of reflection toward activity and therefore on the dependence of activity on social relations. When the movement of activity toward reflection is the object of theoretical attention, when the focus is on *what* people are doing independently of what their behavior means, the operative term is "structure." "Practice" retains the full sense of a dialectic since it points to the contribution of activity to the social relations that make it possible; "structure" extracts one aspect and fixes it in the theoretical form of what Marx called an "abstraction" (Marx 1973, p. 101). The proper critical use of the abstraction of an aspect of something (for example, labor from production, or exploitation from the capitalist mode of production) demonstrates its dependence upon the context from which it has been momentarily isolated or made abstract (such as the problems created for productive activity by its dependence on a price-making money market). This involves showing how the abstracted content fails, on its own account, to achieve independent form and self-determination.

The critical abstraction of structure permits specific implications of an argument to be explored as if the phenomenon in question had no historical aspect. It normally assumes a fixation of practice, or at least segregates what would otherwise be self-reflecting activity from the context that gives it focus and resistence. While this poses a danger of reifying activity, treating it like a thing, it can draw attention to possibilities that might otherwise be ignored: for example, that political or economic domination may have become sufficiently hegemonic to override the normal self-transformative dialectic of practice. In fact, it is from this point of view that researchers have been able to develop empirical evidence about the development and character of contemporary forms of official control whose force derives from decentered authority (cf. Foucault 1977).

The plausibility of such accounts depends upon two rhetorical features of structural analysis: 1. its depiction of domination as virtually complete, and 2. its distinction between "deep" and "surface" effects on community (cf. Horkheimer and Adorno 1972; Marcuse 1964; Habermas 1970b; for theoretical discussions of "cultural hegemony" see Williams 1977; Eagleton 1983; and Laclau and Mouffe 1985). Studies of "deep" effects emphasize "culture" and "symbol." Those of "surface" effects typically refer to the results of coercion and persuasion, in particular the capacity of apparatuses of official control to establish statistically representable regularities among people and activities by holding social relations, and therefore practice, in abeyance (cf. Wolfe 1973; Brown and Goldin 1973; Althusser 1971; Foucault 1973).

Occasionally, structural analysis is used to depict an interest in terms of a possibly permanent intention, one that resists experience. This is often part of refuting claims that a particular interest has universal validity, and typically takes the form of showing that its universal extension requires the suppression of competing interests.

Marx's parody of the market mentality, in the section of *Capital* entitled "The Fetishism of the Commodity and Its Secret," illustrates the demystifying function of critical structuralism (Marx 1976, chapter 1, part 4; cf. Brown 1983–84). Contemporary political theories that describe "the state" as the mutual articulation of institutions and governing agencies illustrate its speculative or projective function (cf. Miliband 1969).

Marx's "deconstruction" of market relations shows that an exclusive interest in the exchange of goods (the universalization of exchange) entails a society consisting of relations among things rather than people:

> Whence, then, arises the enigmatic character of the product of labour, as soon as it assumes the form of a commodity? Clearly, it arises from this form itself. The equality of the kinds of human labour takes on a physical form in the equal objectivity of the products of labour as values; the measure of the expenditure of human labour-power by its duration takes on the form of the magnitude of the value of the products of labour; and finally the relationships between the producers, within which the social characteristics of their labours are manifested, take on the form of a social relation between the products of labour. [Marx 1976, p. 164]

In the case of theories of "the state," the successful domination of society by capital is shown to require a rigid and only partially self-reproducing system of control eventuating in self-defeating escalations of force, and ultimately futile attempts to dominate the means of communication without destroying the social relations that make communication at all possible (cf. Miliband 1977; Habermas 1973, 1975; O'Connor 1973; Davis 1980b; Jessop 1982).

Regardless of the critical usefulness of structural analysis, Marxism remains a theory in relation to practice. As a consequence, the Marxian conception of history must be distinguished from other accounts. It is not the record of past events, a narrative of adventures and conquests, an ordering of territories by the relative advance or regress of their regimes according to standards of "national development," a register of events, a series of structures or formations, or the realization of purposes through increasingly inclusive levels of "social integration." History formulates the dynamic aspect of a society—the tensions that move social relations in regard to themselves—rather than models a society's memory or summarizes its experience.

Economics, as the critique of capital, refers to the interaction of the production and circulation of goods, services, social arrangements, and values. At its most abstract, Marxian economics focuses on the mutual but contradictory and therefore self-transforming articulation of capitalist production with the circulation of "value," the relationship of productive activity to the exchange of goods and money within an expanding, transnational market. Because Marxism understands economy as part of the historical dynamic of society, the Marxian emphasis on it has illuminated a number of otherwise opaque phenomena: the division in everyday life between domestic and wealth-producing activity, the relationship between particular struggles and the generalized struggle of classes, and the often paradoxical relationships between theory and ideology, interest and practice, and state and capital.

This brief preliminary discussion of concepts suggests several working hypotheses: 1. Capitalism can be characterized as a virtual but not actual unity of practice, what Marx called a "mode of production;" 2. This unity can be understood in terms of certain generalized social relations, initially the problematic interdependencies of "class;" 3. The analysis of capitalism requires a definite but qualified detachment from strictly local affairs so that they may be understood in terms of the mediating influences of their contexts; 4. Capitalism can only be understood as a whole from the perspective of those who have no choice but to experience it as a greater unity that includes their immediate circumstances; 5. The perspective of that unity is only possible for labor taken as a class, for those whose survival and well-being depend upon the continual, obligatory, and unconditional sale of their capacity to work for whatever purpose capital's market imposes upon them; 6. The only "actual" unity possible under capitalism is that of labor.

Theory, Bias, and Partisanship: The Problem of Perspective

The last three points assume an argument that will be developed in subsequent chapters. For now they remain working hypotheses with an important methodological implication: the theory of how capitalism works and changes has a decidedly partisan look, and this has led some critics to argue that it is little more than the ideological expression of a special interest. But the bias only appears to be the result of partisanship.

In order to conceptualize the unity of capitalism—indeed, of any arrangement of human affairs—it is necessary to establish the perspective from which that unity can be perceived and the relevant empirical implications tested. To avoid the perspective is to ignore the phenomenon. What appears to be partisanship in the bias of Marxism is rather the orientation of theory within the only perspective from which the theory of capitalism as such can be conceived.

Consider the options. The practical situation of any instance of capital consists of competitive interactions and the immediate constraints of local circumstances on competition for profit. The essential rational operations that we identify with the imperatives of capital are uncritically abstractive in that they must exclude reference to all but the most immediate contexts of the problem of expanding a unit of capital. Capital's perspective, such as it is, is therefore inevitably hostile to analyses of the unity of capitalism. On the other hand, the practical situation of labor is the integration of effort (cooperation) imposed on it to maximize its ability to create wealth. While a fuller discussion of this is undertaken in later chapters, it is at least intuitively plausible that the full scale of capital interactions influences every sale by a worker of his or her capacity to work and every application of hired labor to a profitable task. Assuming that the full discussion makes the case, labor's is the only perspective from which capitalism can be studied as a whole; therefore any theory of capitalism as such will be biased in favor of that perspective to the extent to which it is an authentic theory of the virtual unity of capitalism.

There are two important arguments that can be made against this postion, given the limitations of its preliminary formulation. *First,* the two perspectives may not be exhaustive; there may be a third, or more, superior to both. *Second,* a combination of perspectives may be superior to any one taken alone. The first argument typically invokes the administrative perspective of "rational" management now separated from ownership and work: modern management, even during the nineteenth century, is said to be inevitably situated between state policy and the most general and insistent aspects of the money market; it therefore appears to represent the most universal perspective on capitalism that is historically possible. But this is true only if management is indeed free of the immediate constraints of making profit and is genuinely dissociated from the imperatives of ownership, and if the state is independent of the market, and if the state and the market are themselves the most fundamental features of capitalism. Evidence does not support the first two points, and the third and fourth assume an analysis that has never been done.

The second argument assumes that a known list of perspectives (partial truths) exhausts a higher truth already established as necessary to those partial truths, that they can be combined without changing their content and thereby losing their part of the higher truth, that there are no other partial truths more significant than those combined, and that the higher truth is both known as such to a reason free of perspective and implicit in perspectives that lack such reason.

The ideas of a higher truth of this sort and the sufficiency of a received set of partial truths to the higher truth take us beyond the pale of acceptable epistemology and must be disregarded if for no other reason. Moreover, in the absence of a convincing demonstration of the logical possibility of combining perspectives without losing the partial truths they provide, we have little choice but to proceed as if they must remain distinct. In any case, the argument begs the point: labor's is not merely one perspective among a list of arbitrarily chosen or received possibilities; because "labor" refers to socialized production, people working together, and no other perspective refers to so general a societal fact, it is at least valid prima facie that labor is the only perspective that can recognize the virtual unity of what we call "capitalism."

It may well be that it is not necessary to account for the unity of capitalism or the possibility of such a unity; but if we wish even to entertain such an account, if we wish to study capitalism as such, we have little choice but to do so from the perspective from which that unity is at least conceivable. The alternatives are to study the momentary affairs of particular "entrepreneurs," markets as mechanisms for enabling "fortunes" to expand or contract, the joys and sufferings of particular "employees," or something else that could only be selected for study in the first place because unity is presupposed as the basis of its significance. To reject the possibility of a capitalist unity is, then, not only a result but a cause of the rejection of the perspective of labor. It follows, as well, that the failure to articulate the perspective of labor in the social sciences is an evasion of an obligation to theorize about capitalism and not merely an expression of scientific detachment.

What is at stake is not a point of view but the phenomenon itself. The evasion marks the contemporary discipline of academic economics and its adjacent disciplines as ideological in the sense of abstract ideas that disguise their particularistic interests. Above all, it betrays the primary mission that economists themselves often claim to have undertaken. To articulate labor's perspective is, then, to do more than correct an error or fill a gap. It is to undertake a sociology that embraces economics but assigns to it the status of a subordinate and highly compromised discipline in the social scientific analysis of capitalism.

Summary and Prospects

Marxism is the theory of capitalism from the standpoint of those who make it work but do not receive its rewards. It is sociological to the extent to which it establishes this standpoint as that of society itself, thereby redefining "work" as collective rather than individual action and "rewards" as collective resource rather than competitive gain. Its success as sociology depends upon the demonstration of several key propositions, to be discussed throughout the remainder of this book: 1. the accumulation of wealth by private parties depends upon a general exploitation of human labor; 2. the anarchic competition that characterizes capitalist accumulation inevitably translates wealth into power and power into pervasive domination; 3. accumulatable wealth, wealth that can retain its value and grow, requires forms of social organization that private accumulation cannot sustain; 4. consequently, the "struggle of classes" in modern capitalism reflects a more fundamental antagonism than is typically acknowledged of capitalist economy and the society of that economy.

These propositions challenge prevailing assumptions about the nature and origin of what is ordinarily recognized as "wealth," and offer a critique of standard theories in terms of their ideological aspect and the material interests that they defend. The challenge lies in the distinction between the socially useful wealth that we think of as a necessary resource for the maintenance of societal order, democratic participation, and cooperation, and the individualized control over tokens, things, and people that service the antisocietal interest of the controlling class. The critique attempts to penetrate the deceptions of the ostensible social order, to disclose the interests whose disposition is exploitive of people and hostile to society, and to identify the most general problem capitalism poses to the society upon which it depends.

The Marxian tradition has produced a number of important findings that indicate the range of connection between society and economy. The following list completes this introduction:

1. Capitalism divides its usable populations into classes that represent its essential productive operations.

2. It encourages the establishment of sanctioned and differentially privileged activities that reinforce the economic and political dominance of one class, capital, over the other, labor.

3. The history of capitalist development institutes a culture where all things are valued according to abstract standards of comparison, founded upon the exchangeability of things on the market rather than on their suitability to human needs and sociality.

4. Its history necessarily includes the progressive degrading of labor by the mechanization, standardization, and routinization of work, by an increasing separation of work from personal and group life, and by the steady reduction of human control in all activities related to production.

5. Capital attempts, so far as it is able, to organize the whole of society as a resource for the private accumulation of wealth.

6. Private control over socially produced wealth undermines the democratic institutions and principles that capitalists nevertheless claim to reinforce, and the development of such control undermines the "free" market and the principle of competition upon which capitalism allegedly depends.

7. The attempt by capital to manage the affairs of its society paradoxically involves the creation of social, political, economic, and cultural forces opposed to it.

8. The crises of capitalism arise from tendencies inherent in it and result in transformations that are, at least momentarily, incompatible with the private accumulation of wealth.

9. Everything that can be identified as part of the development and transformation of capitalism expresses the class struggle that is its historically decisive feature.

10. Socialism is the progressive socialization of the means of producing what society needs. It ratifies and attempts to sustain what capital itself had created—cooperative labor and enjoyment—and opposes the antisocial tendencies inherent in systems of private ownership of socially necessary means of production.

The following chapters discuss the arguments from which these propositions are derived and explore their significance for a Marxian sociology.

Note

1. "It is a false abstraction to treat a nation whose mode of production is based on value, and organized capitalistically into the bargain, as a unified body simply working for the national needs" (Marx 1981b, p. 991).

3

Marxian Theory

Marxism is not a framework for interpretation or social commentary though it can be and has been used for both; nor can it be understood as an attempt to provide a natural science of human affairs. Its claim to constitute an authentic human science depends upon three criteria: 1. the adequacy of what it produces as knowledge to a conception of humanity as capable of producing knowledge; 2. the identification of phenomena within contexts sufficiently diversified to establish their complexity and significance; 3. the completeness with which historically significant social relations are incorporated in theoretical concepts.

In accepting the interpenetration of science and philosophy, Marxian theory not only studies the human world of self-creating practice, it establishes the historical conditions of that study by asserting in all respects the interdependence of knowledge and practice, and by clarifying in each instance the historical conditions under which that interdependence can be represented from the standpoint of knowledge.[1]

To the extent that it attempts to establish the objectivity of the experience of capitalism, Marxian theory shows how the phenomena of that experience—events, arrangements, and things—become objectively significant in the social relations and practices of absolutely competing interests. "Interest" refers to a collectively significant practice from the point of view of its possible universalization. It therefore refers to an intention, or intentionality, within a field of opposing intentions or intentionalities.

"Objective reality" consists of all that is appropriate to, noticeable within, and marked by the self-directed, or practical, actions of collectivities in situations of conflict. "Practice" refers to acts that are in one way or another, but not deliberately enunciated as, directed toward the resubstantiation of an interest. Practice is, in other words, collective activity understood from the point of view of its orientation to itself as a possible universalization; it is collective activity that attempts to assert itself—collectivity—against an equally insistent opposition. It follows that Marxism clarifies a realm of objectivity that is already a human accomplishment and an index of collective interest.

THEORY AS CRITICAL PRACTICE

The Marxian project involves three interrelated types of critique: the *critique of objects* in regard to their subjective significance, the *historicizing or historical critique of the subjectivity that organizes objects* according to their significance, and the *critique of ideology* that distinguishes practical and nonpractical aspects of theory.

Critique of Objects

The first type of critique aims to show that the significance of objects depends upon their relevance to the possible realization of interests. Its theoretical self-consciousness, its relation to practice, is evident in the forms by which it displays its own basis in interest—that is, the forms in which its own objects are identified. Without that relation to practice, critique would merely be a symptom, the helpless projection of a concern, in a word, ideology. Symptomatic critique lacks the self-reflecting intentionality, the reference to itself, that otherwise enables it to account for what it has overcome in order to produce its result and therefore to be able to learn and teach (cf. Blum and McHugh 1984).

The following case illustrates the distinction between self-conscious and symptomatic critical practice. People often vote in national elections as part of a ritualized—accepted but unintended—realization of citizenship. Voting is, conventionally, an "elevated" act that needs no further justification than the fact that it is done. Enthusiasm for voting depends on the convenience of its moral achievement rather than the resolution of personal tension good works are said normally to accomplish. To vote is rarely to subject citizenship as such to critical scrutiny.

There are, however, cases in which voting displays an authenticity of commitment in its most immediately interpretable aspect. For example, a vote for a third party in a political milieu hostile to dissent may assert itself against that milieu rather than merely in regard to the issues and personalities of the election that normally take the situation for granted. As such, the act can be said to display the history of its own decisiveness as a feature of its socially valid subjectivity. Symptomatic voting offers nothing in prospect and realizes nothing for the memory of self. It has nothing to teach, no project to fulfill, no growth to record. It merely fulfills a duty to which one had never agreed. Voting as a critical act is persuasive because it displays the tension of choice and within that tension respect for the temptation of alternatives that must be overcome if the act is to be socially realized as a valid representation of a self.

Voting as a matter of duty may appear, but then only in retrospect, to be an attempt to influence "the balance of power." But because it is virtually inconceivable that an individual vote could wield such influence and doubtful that a reasonable person would have assumed so in the first place, to claim that power is a vote's purpose can hardly persuade others to vote. This extreme polarization of convenience and critique within a single act may account for some of the peculiar rhetorical features of strictly political discourses—that is, that they tend to be at best irrepressibly ironical and at worst moralizing, formulaic, and glib. On the other hand, the critical vote disturbs what are often taken for granted as fixed conditions and permanent obligations or ideologically induced delusions of power. The form of its enactment—that it uses conventional means to break the frame of conventionality—is seditious, and therefore regardless of content it is likely to be seen as dramatic and exemplary (cf. Martin 1985). It forces people to account for mundane activities that are normally convenient or incorrigible in other respects.

There is this critical aspect to all human activity. Everything we do can be understood as expressing the ambiguity of conditions and uncertainties of meaning, and a corresponding ambivalence toward what is normally convenient (in the moral sense) in our activities (cf. Goffman 1961a, 1963). Because of this, every act can be seen as containing something of a challenge, a small rebellion, the possibility of reflection and change. When this is admitted to awareness, when it is socially and discursively realized, we refer to the admission as intellectual work, protest, dissent, and so on. Indeed, the analysis of human action in terms of its critical aspect (or the possibility of such an aspect) is epistemologically essential to the Marxian project (cf. Habermas 1970b, 1971). It is a condition for realizing any theory of knowledge that hopes to reconcile theory and practice.

Critique of Subjectivity

The critique of subjectivity demonstrates the conflict that underlies the expression of an interest. This form of significance depends on the fact that, unlike private motives or unsocialized needs that require only gratification and then reiterate their demands as if nothing had occurred, interests are virtually exclusive and comprehensive claims on a whole order of activity the elements of which thereby achieve their relevance (cf. Schutz 1970). Such claims are only conceivable if there are alternatives, or at least the prospect of alternatives. The formulation and realization of any interest presuppose, then, the presence of totally different and thus contradictory interests (cf. Ollman 1971). In other words, an interest is practical only to the extent to which its instances can be shown to display the tension of the oppositions it presumes to resolve (Blum and McHugh 1984).

Psychoanalysis illustrates the logic of this critique applied to the theoretical form we call "personality." It shows that what appears to be a structured whole is actually a contradictory interaction of something on the order of "interests." In this way it demonstrates the historical character of its object. For this example to be an appropriate illustration, "interests" must refer to essential but competing claims upon the individual's total development that can legitimately be said to be internal to that development (cf. Habermas 1971; Sartre 1976).

Psychoanalysis argues that the maturation of a personality involves the progressive achievement of self-control through the management of the body and the appraisal and reappraisal of situations. The imperative of self-control operates like an interest in its historical significance to the development and realization of personality. However, this exclusive and comprehensive claim on personality, this demand for total order in the self, can only be realized as a demand if there is something to regulate that develops in its own terms, constantly poses the problem of regulation, and establishes the priority of process to structure that is essential if personality is to reflect the creativity we require of anything we call "human." For psychoanalysis, this totally different, contradictory, and necessary "interest" is need or impulse; and it appears, from the standpoint of the competing "interest" in self-control, as irrational.

If the history at issue is that of personality, then what the person does in regard to events, arrangements, and things must be understood as reflecting exclusive and comprehensive interests in self-control and the immediate achievement of pleasure (the indulgence of impulse or need). This is why Freud used metaphors of war and politics to characterize this ego-mediated "class struggle" of the mind. The history of the individual personality is the struggle between and transformation of "interests" that contend for the same space. Without both "interests" there is neither the tense virtual formation we call "personality" nor anything that can be called "personality development." Given both, there is a continual struggle registered, often beyond awareness, as uneasiness, ambivalence, defensiveness, obsessiveness, and an ungovernable volatility in activity itself.

What keeps this from resolving itself in repetitious behavior or wild swings between extremes is the fact, bracketed by psychoanalysis in order to foreground the struggle, that the individual is imbedded in a social reality that mediates his or her life as thoroughly as if it too were internal to personality. In other words, "personality" is an abstraction from a more complex set of affairs designed to highlight the historical character of even the most minute unit of analysis and therefore the creativity, impetuousness, and sociality of the agencies of work and exchange that record themselves as individuals. Without this, there would be no aspect of self that could reach beyond the limitations of situations, no basis for the essential communion through which the community of interest beyond the individual achieves the status of practice and the society of interests achieves its fundamental historical character.

These are the terms in which psychoanalysis is consistent with the Marxian critique of capitalism, both for what it supplies by way of its critique of individuality and for its exemplification of critical logic applied to a phenomenon normally thought exempt from it (cf. Jacoby 1975; Habermas 1970b; Brown 1979b).

From this point of view, psychotherapy is the revolutionary moment within the person. It is possible because of the social character of personality, the essential incompleteness of the individual. It is necessary because the divisions within personality cannot be reconciled without the mediation of social relations. The success of therapy is gauged by the individual's recognition of his or her helplessness to the internal struggle of impulse and control, the necessity of both and their essentially contradictory character, and the importance of existential social commitments to their mediation. Ultimately, therapy succeeds to the extent to which the alienation of the individual's internal life is superceded by its reemergence in the history of collectivities and by his or her awareness of that transformation reconstituted as a socially valid awareness of the collective practice of its achievement.

Psychotherapy presupposes a society that is itself an arena of contradiction and struggle. Therapy is part of an endless dialectic of socialization and resistance that involves linguistic, instrumental, and expressive activities significant to the further development and extension of collective life. We will examine some of the implications of this type of critique in a later chapter in regard to the problems of class consciousness and ideology. For now the discussion is sufficient to illustrate the logic of historical critique. That it suggests as well the possibility of a Marxian social psychology is a topic for further discussion.

Critique of Ideology

The critique of ideology resembles in some respects symptomatic activity. While it has something in common with what is normally called criticism, it retains the historical perspective of the critique of capital. Its aim is to expose the ideological aspect of what otherwise appear to be absolute objectivity in theory, detachment and neutrality in the conduct of research, and collectively valid representation in policy.

"Ideology" refers in this critique to a set of image-focused propositions that can only be realized as ideas in unreflective discourse. They are essentially symptomatic of but not reflexive to practice: they have the quality of epiphenomena that can be used as received but never brought by that use fully to critical notice. As central figures of a mode of discourse whose momentum eludes self-criticism, they remain in memory as, at most, a fixed moral residue, like school grades or a bank balance. Their use involves placing them in ostensibly rational discourses made up of connections among already processed dehistoricizing unities—abstractions like "common sense," "reason," "decency," "patriotism," "our nation"—in a way that reinforces their discursive convenience independently of and in opposition to the quality of argument. For example, the contemporary propaganda of "national security" evokes the yet more generalized sense of a potential violation of family and settlement by dramatizing the threat as the defilement of innocence by something irrepressibly corrupt. It draws its immediate force from analogies of "enemies" to more commonplace domestic villains, of "the threat" to the flagrant violations of personal security ordinarily associated with rape, betrayal, and abuse, and of "the nation" to meek creatures of good will, enormous forebearance, and potentially devastating power.

Innocence, violation, forebearance, and heroism are figures of an even more pervasive imagination. They lie deep in the unreflective discourses of a variety of topical moralities—child rearing, patriotism, and treason, the betrayal of tradition, the disciplines of crime and sex—and they elevate their participants to a moral position immune to allegations of confusion, frustration, and futility (cf. Foucault, 1980). Their use is automatic to those discourses and in the ordinary case relatively harmless. But when deployed in official propaganda to justify policies that would otherwise lack foundation, coherence, or value, they are capable of great immediate harm: witness the consistent use of such propaganda by American presidents during the past decades to justify militarism in foreign policy and to rationalize the class- and race-biased management of domestic populations. The innocence and forebearance of hard-working Americans, the perversity and violence of terrorists, communism, and the Third World, and the myth of the hero's stand, pervade the public media and convey an overwhelming sense of validity and concreteness to official outrage. They reinforce a desecularization of polity and honor in the affairs of state. They give to politics its current moralistic flair and to politicians the imagic resources to preach rather than persuade.

The technical application of the critique of ideology to the established disciplines (as in recent critiques of psychology, history, literary theory, and economics) is not intended to refute their specific claims so much as to situate those claims within the social relations that make them possible. It is intended to show that received ideas and the theories they support are to some extent symptomatic, that they cannot account for the history of which they are a part without contradicting themselves (cf. Gouldner 1970, 1976; Williams 1977; Eagleton 1983; Habermas, 1970a, Han 1979).

The point is not that ideas are true only when they provide an absolute and permanently valid explanation of human affairs; it is rather that an interest in knowing *society* only arises when there is reason to question the bases of action, and such reasons can arise only in a context of conflicts that make *knowledge* a matter of selection rather than certainty and *knowing* a matter of urgency rather than the passive receipt of information. This is an historical point. Whatever we mean by "knowledge," it is something that reflects upon and resolves collectively significant differences. It follows that knowledge is always limited by practice. Therefore, the validity of any theoretical claim depends in part on a critical exposure of the differences it resolves and the conflicts for which it is practical and hence an instance of knowledge.

Those differences and conflicts may, on the other hand, be disguised by the form or content of a theoretical proposal. Empirical statements in the form of lawlike propositions are ideological unless they are qualified by reference to an interest in a context of interests and thus by the political interactions in which they resolve conflict. Their referents are ideological unless they are shown to have contradictory aspects that correspond to the conflict in which they emerge as issues, unless they are shown to be objects of significant dispute (cf. Habermas, 1971).

Marxism is no more exempt from the critique of ideology than other theories. Its advantage is the self-criticism that is part of its method. As we will see, the universal character of labor's interest is historically compromised by the lack of universalism implicit in the capitalism for which a theory of collectivities, interests, practices, and contradictions is appropriate.

Labor's interest in a society without exploitation is universal only within the context of exploitive social relations. It does not follow from this, however, that capital represents an authentic alternative interest in society. Indeed, capital is inconceivable without the exploitation of labor, yet it requires that exploitation be absent as a concept from theory. That is the paradox of capitalist social science that marks it as ideological and gives Marxism one important occasion for its critique of ideology.

The most direct method available for the critique of ideology involves 1. extracting referential terms from the discourses in which their use is convenient, and 2. identifying a possible history of that usage. This requires reading through terms and statements to the underlying conflicts that they appear to resolve and by that resolution disguise (cf., for example, Eagleton 1983; Brown 1983–84; Blum and McHugh 1984).

The use of received names for things, in a discourse in which statements made about them do not allow what is implicit in the naming to be called into question, encourages their independent objectivity to be taken for granted. This in turn reinforces the independent momentum, or fluency, of the discourse and the illusion created by that momentum of consensus among speakers. This objectification is part of the dialectic of discourse; but without some sort of intervention, it defeats the possibility of speakers' recognizing, at the moment that they are certain in what they say of what they know, that certainty is the result of a selection from among incompatible aspects of things according to incompatible interests. The convenience of speech, its fluency, its ordinariness, is the primary object of the critique of ideology; and it can only be disturbed by insisting that usage be taken seriously and called to account for itself despite the fact that this violates the momentum discourse requires if it is to be socially viable (Brown 1983–84).

This principle can be illustrated by an example from the history of sociology. Early theorists of "organizations" and "groups" typically identified their phenomenon by referring to collections of people whose unity seemed beyond question due to their collective reputations, the fact that they could be named conveniently, or the fact that they had become objects of official recognition (cf. Brown and Goldin 1973— ethnicities, riots, industrial enterprises, publics, and neighborhoods are examples). From this identification it was possible to formulate hypotheses about the forms and contents of interaction, the relationship between task characteristics and decision-making, styles of leadership, satisfaction and "performance," reactions to "deviance," and the cyclical movement of solidarity and task-orientation that seemed to characterize the culture of collective life, appropriate to integral or "boundary maintaining" formations. When the facts were recalcitrant, distinctions were introduced between, for example, "formal organization" and "informal organization," "role" and "performance," "competence" and "deviance," "socialized behavior" and "spontaneous contribution," "goals" and "definitions of the situation," "social structure" and "emergent norms." In each case, the first member of the pair idealized a reputed unity; the second represented the ad hoc use of a relatively unrationalized concept to account for the fact that disunity was as apparent as unity. But unity remained the presupposition of analysis and disunity and conflict the noisy factors that seemed more to reflect external than internal influences (Brown 1978; Bittner 1965).

The upshot was a reduction of the concept of "social action" to rationalistic idealizations of "science" (the technical appropriateness of means) and "exchange" (the standardization of ends). This gave "rational decision" the status of a paradigm (Parsons 1949; March and Simon 1958). But the abstraction of process from the contexts in which process bears on social relations effectively disguised the particularism of interest represented by the paradigm (cf. Gouldner 1970; Habermas 1970a). In the extreme case, science as technique, and exchange as the exchange of money and commodities, came to represent the result of what Parsons referred to as the "law" of the progressive rationalization of social affairs (1949).

On the other hand, the idealization of an essentially market-oriented rationality provided an opportunity to reevaluate the history of popular movements, riots, and protest. Once observer bias was taken into account (cf. Turner 1964), it became possible to argue that "collective behavior" was more rational than had previously been supposed: at least in terms of the processes of legitimation, decision, the mobilization of resources, the specification of roles, and the responsiveness to situations that could be found in the midst of what otherwise appeared to be chaos.

But the application of the paradigm merely reproduced for social movements the original distinction that had been invidious to them. In effect, it attempted to conventionalize what was unconventional by separating the "rational" kernel from the "irrational" fringe and by placing the "content" of protest in the context of institutional procedures for solving problems, as if that "content" were not in some other sense contradictory to the interests supported by those procedures. The result of the rationalization in theory of what seemed to have been hopelessly irrational was, to be sure, a certain amount of sympathy for the claims of dissenting groups; but it nevertheless supported policies of compromise through institutional regulation that begged the question of what interests were supported by such regulation. From the standpoint of the movements, it was as if the interests of the competing parties represented no serious differences of power, and as if they could be combined by extending the rationality of officially-established institutions to include all the parties, leaving the unfulfilled demands— the unassimilatable content—on the side of the irrational.

The normative implication of the theory was twofold: on the one hand, to resist compromise was irrational; on the other, to accept compromise while still maintaining a position of antagonism consistent with conflict required accepting the intervention of detached arbitrators capable of transcending the conflict altogether for the sake of its rational resolution. In other words, "Reason" required the suspension of one's own reason in favor of another's, a condition that has not proven fruitful in the actual engagements of social movements with their opposition and that has often proven disastrous when accepted by those whose lack of power gave negotiation a different meaning for them than it had for their opposition (cf. Brown and Goldin 1973; Piven and Cloward 1982).

Both the model and the policy reconfirmed the idea of a basic unity in society that was neither tested nor subjected to critical review. Moreover, each disguised the character or the conflict that motivated the assumption of unity in the first place, and took for granted that the parties in interest could be identified sociologically by the same collective names used in ordinary and official discourses (cf. Brown and Goldin 1973). One ironical implication was that "membership" connoted an institutionally relevant "citizenship" that combined, for example, workers and businessmen, slum dwellers and affluent suburbanites, and officials and civilians. Yet the logic of naming and ordering names that was inherent in the organization-theoretic rationalistic idealization of social movements could only end by denying the rationality of those for whom names were merely names.

It was as if what registrars call "the student body" is a body in fact, or what pollsters call "public opinion" is the reflection of a group. One does not refer to a "society" by naming a territory, a "group" by naming an assembly or collection, or a "social system" by registering as "authority" the power that some have over others.

Juridically recognized corporations such as AT&T, General Motors, Columbia University, the City of New York, the Catholic Church, and the Democratic Party, are not necessarily collectivities. Their unity is a matter of reputation or is formally conferred by agencies interested in the allocation of rights, obligations, or powers. It is a unity primarily of administrative convenience, not one achieved in the play of competing interests or even one that extends a line of development from a "primary" situation such as settlement, voluntary agreement, or the requirements of a shared task (cf. Bittner 1965; Brown, 1978).

The social unity of such entities is, for the critique of ideology, illusory. Yet much of what still passes for the sociology of organizations accepts the illusion and continues at best to reduce the operations of such entities to romanticized "primary situations," conflating qualitatively different sorts of sociality, such as the family, the business firm, the university, government, territorial areas, social movements, armies, nations, and ethnic assemblies.

Given this move, it became possible to interpret statistical relations among "variables" as indicating variants of solidarity, culture, or functional interdependence, though such relations could as easily indicate the capacity of certain centers of power momentarily to fix social practices (cf. Goffman 1961a). Marxian critics of this literature usually favor this later hypothesis, as current research on the composition and recomposition of the workforce illustrates (cf., for example, Gordon, et al. 1982; Harvey 1973). In any case, there seems to be little willingness among radical social scientists to accept the presumptions that national societies are analogous to the extended family or that there is a rational and inspired social order to capitalism that well-socialized reasoning subjects constantly attempt to implement and celebrate in their daily activities.

The convenience of received or assigned names to the sociology of organizations has begged fundamental questions about the history and contradictions of what appear to be unified social formations, about the character of what appear to be deviant or untoward acts, and about the nature of the "mechanisms" by which "membership" and "participation" are instituted and their "functionality" to "organizational" operations made apparent. The critique of ideology intervenes in this discourse by insisting that terms be taken seriously for the concepts, images, and perspectives they make available. What it emphasizes is not so much the presence of error as the inability of theorists such as those of the "organization" genre to transcend the particularisms of the interests whose perspectives they articulate (Lazarsfeld 1967a).

THEORY AS INTERVENTION

The capacity of the critical project to learn and teach depends upon the respect it shows for alternative positions. Consequently, Marxian theory must be understood as an intervention in rather than a disruption or immediate supercession of the discourse it criticizes. It begins, one might say, phenomenologically rather than hermeneutically, *within* the language its critique ultimately shows to be ideological.[2]

The first passages of Marx's *Capital* read as follows:

> The wealth of societies in which the capitalist mode of production prevails appears as an "immense collection of commodities"; the individual commodity appears as its elementary form. Our investigation therefore begins with the analysis of the commodity.
> The commodity is, first of all, an external object, a thing which through its qualities satisfies human needs of whatever kind. [Marx 1976, p. 125]

It is clear from this that Marx intends to guide rather than confront his reader (cf. Brown 1983–84). These passages express a specific idealizing perspective that takes for granted the thing-like quality and collectibility of commodities and the reasonableness of representing them as objects that satisfy human needs and, through that capacity, comprise the wealth of societies. The position is that of a "bourgeois," mired in the discourses of property, goods, and exchange, and the illusions of rational production on a national scale taken also as the scale of a society. Marx's use of the term "appears" acknowledges that it is a compelling position if only because of the conventional simplicity with which it takes for granted the elementary and local forms of commerce.

The fact that this position is offered as a tempting one establishes it as an authentic option to the critical perspective that Marx hopes to illuminate, and shows that work needs to be done if he is to succeed. Ultimately, he will offer nothing more novel than what emerges in the course of his internal critique of the logic and discourses of capital. What makes this an internal critique is the method by which Marx unravels that logic and those discourses, a method that begins by taking terms more seriously than their ordinary use permits, thereby making conflict apparent even before it becomes explicit.

A conflict can only be made explicit by acts that participate in it, that contribute practically to the historical process it signifies (cf. Williams 1975, 1977, 1980; Althusser 1970; Thompson 1978; Anderson 1980). Marxian theory operates within the practical context of the class struggle that it brings to notice. It functions as a reflective intervention in discourses that it shows to be strategically relevant to that struggle.

Once terms have been taken seriously, it is necessary to identify difference where there appeared to be unity and to establish the phenomenological foundation for the appearance of unity where there is difference. Thus,

> Commodities come into the world in the form of use-values or material goods. . . . This is their plain, homely, natural form. However, they are only commodities because they have a dual nature, because they are at the same time objects of utility and bearers of value. Therefore they only appear as commodities, or have the form of commodities, in so far as they possess a double form, i.e. natural form and value form. . . . However, let us remember that commodities possess an objective character as values only in so far as they are all expressions of an identical social substance, human labour, that their objective character as values is therefore purely social. [Marx 1976, pp. 138–9]
>
> The internal opposition between use-value and value, hidden within the commodity, is therefore represented on the surface by an external opposition, i.e. by a relation between two commodities such that the one commodity, *whose own* value is supposed to be expressed, counts directly only as a use-value, whereas the other commodity, *in which* that value is

to be expressed, counts directly only as exchange-value. Hence the simple form of value of a commodity is the simple form of appearance of the opposition between use-value and value which is contained within the commodity. [ibid., p. 153].

It is only by being exchanged that the products of labour acquire a socially uniform objectivity as values, which is distinct from their sensuously varied objectivity as articles of utility. This division of the product of labour into a useful thing and a thing possessing value appears in practice only when exchange has already acquired a sufficient extension and importance to allow useful things to be produced for the purpose of being exchanged, so that their character as values has already to be taken into consideration during production. From this moment on, the labour of the individual producer acquires a twofold social character. On the one hand, it must, as a definite useful kind of labour, satisfy a definite social need, and thus maintain its position as an element of the total labour, as a branch of the social division of labour, which originally sprang up spontaneously. On the other hand, it can satisfy the manifold needs of the individual producer himself only in so far as every particular kind of useful private labour can be exchanged with, i.e. counts as the equal of, every other kind of useful private labour. Equality in the full sense between different kinds of labour can be arrived at only if we abstract from their real inequality, if we reduce them to the characteristic they have in common, that of being the expenditure of human labour-power, of human labour in the abstract. The private producer's brain reflects this twofold social character of his labour only in the forms which appear in practical intercourse, in the exchange of products. Hence the socially useful character of his private labour is reflected in the form that the product of labour has to be useful to others, and the social character of the equality of the various kinds of labour is reflected in the form of the common character, as values, possessed by these materially different things, the products of labour. [ibid., p. 166].

It is not necessary to discuss at this point the analysis implicit in these conclusions. It is enough to see in them the appearance of difference and opposition and to recognize the transformation that has taken place through the critique of ideology.

Marxian theory specifies the object it studies by identifying the difference implicit in the assertion of its unity. The critique of unity—of the commodity, value, labor—reflects on the subjective aspect of and hence the tension between unity and difference. If the object is an opposition (for example, capitalist production), the subject for which that object is real (that is, the class relation) must be in some sense divided. The "class division of capitalism" is not a division of population but one within consciousness experienced—that is, discursively realized—as the ambiguity of objects. This emphasis on the irreducibility of difference is why Marxian theory cannot be said to aim at imposing "true" ideas on "false" ones and cannot be held to account for "hypotheses" tested in its name. Rather, in exposing difference and opposition, it clarifies the historical dimension of human reality. Like Freudian psychoanalysis, the Marxian critique aims not to satisfy but to enlighten.[3]

THE INTEREST OF MARXISM

But if Marxism disturbs the convenience of categories, it is legitimate to inquire as to its own warrant, its own foundation in interest. Either it is constituted within and limited by a practice or it must defend the claim that there can be a truth beyond history. The question is, from what standpoint, in regard to what interest, in relation to what predicament, as a feature of what practice, can the objectivity of events, arrangements, and things be best understood as a feature of collective action? The answer will depend on the validity of two propositions: 1. society cannot be understood independently of the historical character of capitalist production and its socialization of labor; 2. the generalization of collective action is the foundation of the resources that make society possible.

Marxism articulates an interest in cooperation as the answer to an historic predicament. Capital establishes cooperative production as the basis of its economy: it expands the value of production by socializing its labor force. But the use of that capacity by private parties for the sake of accumulating wealth that they can dispose of as they wish establishes the conflict variously referred to as class struggle, the antagonism of economy to society, or the contradiction between the forces and relations of production. The private exploitation of social labor redefines wealth as investible funds and monetary profit in contrast with and opposition to wealth conceived of as the necessary conditions for the further development of the "society of the producers."

The interest in cooperation has revolutionary implications that capitalists have recognized more often than workers. In order to maintain the society of cooperative production, cooperation that reproduces itself, the disposition of products must be as socially responsible as their production is socially constituted. But since cooperation requires a mobilization of resources inconsistent with the private ownership of the means of production, this social responsibility cannot be guaranteed or even made probable. This inconsistency becomes acutely critical when economy reaches the limits of its political boundaries. This is certainly why capitalist administration so often responds violently to the suggestion of even minimal reforms, and why its theory of social order has no place for political activities aimed at socially oriented economic changes (cf. Wolfe 1973).

Therefore, to the extent that it is the critique of capital, Marxian theory articulates the interest of labor in sustaining a socially responsible productive order. As part of the historical situation referred to by the term "capitalism," Marxism expresses whatever prospect exists from within for perceiving that situation as a whole (cf. Lukács 1971; Lefebvre 1968; Sartre 1976; but cf. Cohen 1979, for a different point of view).

An account of a society from within is necessarily governed by practical considerations (cf. Garfinkel 1967). An account of it as a whole establishes connections between what people do together and the most general interests that can explain what they do. From that point of view, capitalism is a set of mutually incompatible yet mutually sustaining interests in cooperative production. It is only in regard to such contradictory interests that activities that appear to be independent can be shown to be related to one another and therefore to be historically and sociologically significant.

Exploitation and Experience

The ultimate test of Marxian theory is its relevance to the practical activities by which people attempt to improve their society, a test, it must be added, that is never applied after the fact but is a constitutive feature of the theory even at the moment of its most sectoral and tactical (conjunctural) applications. It is reasonable therefore to ask whether individuals and collectivities form self-critical representations of the relationship between what they do and the historical contradiction of totally organizing interests; and it is reasonable to ask how that relationship is reflected in theory.

Ordinary experience, limited by the localism of its situations, registers this relationship as the fate of individuals. People can be aware that what they do depends upon forces beyond their control and direct comprehension; or, to the extent to which we identify people as parties to and actors in situations we must conclude that their sense of what lies beyond the horizon of those situations can only refer to undifferentiated power and therefore to the mystery of such power. Others that lie beyond that horizon are part of its mystery. Therefore, the awareness, the discursive realization, of the relationship of situation to history includes an unavoidable dissociation of self and society, an alienation at the most generalized level of local collective- and self-knowledge.

A poetics of this awareness would certainly refer to a variety of familiar figures: massive determinations of nature, potent and essentially foreign dispositions of energy and purpose, and identifications of scale beyond secular comprehension. These appear in ordinary discourse as nation, economy, government, enemy, market, industry, production, tradition; and they include in each case invidious alters involving failures of citizenship, incompetence or corruption, apathy or disloyalty, cowardice, and inactivity. One can hardly avoid enuciating those unrationalizable abstractions; but they can be spoken only when such speech raises no further questions about them. Marxism attempts to grasp and make comprehensible this sense of a troubled self in a troubling but ineffable world through its "critique of political economy" (Jameson 1981, Williams 1977, Eagleton 1983, Sartre 1963, Habermas 1970b; and cf. Foucault 1973).

If capitalism is a way of organizing social life so that production expands but remains controlled by private parties for a socially restrictive benefit, then two propositions follow: 1. human effort is not exercised in order to serve itself; 2. the expenditure of effort must be controlled in as many respects as possible in order to reduce interference with the private appropriation of the fruits of social production (cf. Marx 1976, appendix, especially p. 990). The first proposition is often expressed as the fact that products are not made under capitalism for the use of those who create them. The second implies that capitalist economy imposes a bias on the polity of its society that corresponds to the negative, antisocial interest of capital. The word that most aptly names this state of affairs is "exploitation"; and it is first recognized— though this is a recognition muted by myth and ideology—as a sense of being overwhelmed by forces as mysteriously fateful and merciless as gods.[4]

To exploit is to use something or someone exclusively for one's own ends. Exploitation, therefore, denies the autonomy of the other, treats him, her, or it as resource rather than value, stratifies relations in such a way that places can never be exchanged, and immunizes the exploiter from the humanity of the exploited and therefore from the principle of humanity itself. While it is not necessary that exploitive acts have these effects, they are inevitable when the whole of society is organized by the exploitation of labor, when the gain of one is always a loss for the many.

The term is also used to refer to the subjective experience of those who objectively serve, to the sense of being dominated by those with whom one has no common purpose but without whom one cannot live. The fact that such a condition denies the relevance of one's own purposes and therefore invalidates one's experience of self, makes it likely that the sense of being exploited will rarely be articulate in speech, though it will always be registered in one way or another.

The experience can be explored phenomenologically, that is, described in terms of principles that organize the ephemera of experience in relation to the self as a field of tense intuition in which details appear to have significance, to be variously centered, and to have a certain urgency or inevitability in their multifarious connections. Exploitation would register itself from that point of view as a sense of being moved, depleted, dependent, replaceable, irrelevant, yet grateful for the small mercies of life. The negative aspect of this experience generalizes from the objective situation; the positive aspect reflects the space that remains for subjectivity and the assignment of worth—worth being tied to the values of the dominant other, subjectivity to the appreciation of that other's ability to yield small mercies.

When it is articulate, the experience of exploitation registers an immediate awareness that one deserves no rights: "because" of being no more than an instance of a type or category, "because" of lacking the capacity for self-evaluation and self-control, "because" of hoping for too much and getting more than one deserves. Such a consciousness longs for utopia past or present, and gauges the moral quality of acts by the standards of unities beyond any grasp. In its expanded form, this experience of the self as desiring but not deserving honesty, loyalty, and respect has its concomitant experience of others as thieves and betrayers of promises (Sartre 1963, 1964; Sennett and Cobb 1972; Lefebvre 1971).

The experience of exploitation has more to it even than this. It tends to generalize beyond its situation, to become a perspective. On the one hand, its irrepressibility indicates the extensiveness of its conditions; on the other, because it is difficult to constrain, to make appropriate, that irrepressibility is itself a minimal subversion of those conditions. Above all, the experience and its irrepressibility are the subjective aspect of objective conditions, part of the dialectic of capitalist accumulation and more generally the capitalist mode of production.

The discussion of exploitation in this chapter has attempted to make a prima facie case for a relationship of reflection/theory to practical activity. But both the subjective and objective aspects of this relationship are only properly represented as aspects of a theoretically constituted phenomenon, in this case capitalist production. It is necessary then to turn from the appeal to intuition to the analysis of the capitalist mode of production.

Notes

1. The interpenetration of philosophy and science has been discussed in various ways by Habermas 1971; Althusser 1970; Ollman 1971; Anderson 1976, 1980; and Cohen 1979. See Laclau and Mouffe 1985, for a recent

critique of political interpretations of that relationship from the point of view of the "deconstructionist" problematic; and see Levine 1984 for a discussion in the context of "arguing for socialism."

2. "Phenomenologically" in the sense of reflecting within the limits of a consciousness and in regard to the commitments entailed by them, but in regard to their possible transcendence.

3. It goes without saying that theory cannot reconcile difference on its own account. It could do so only if it were legitimate to appeal to a preexisting unity of interest that could provide a standard for reconciliation, or if it were to deny the extra-theoretical process of reconciliation that it must nevertheless assume.

4. This is not intended to imply that the theory of exploitation is a theory of individual experience or consciousness. In subsequent chapters, exploitation will be shown to be an objective condition.

4

The Theory of Labor's Capitalism: Origins and Methodology

Several terms are of special importance: *class, labor, productivity, wealth, accumulation,* and *exchange.* Their use predates Marx and the capitalist revolution of industry. They began to appear together as coordinate topics of popular and learned discourse at the beginning of the nineteenth century, when people could speak unequivocally of the affairs they had in common on an entirely new and vast scale (cf. Williams 1980, 1976, 1960; Hobsbawm 1962; Dumont 1977; Foucault 1973). What Eric Hobsbawm refers to as the democratic influence in England of the French Revolution, was also symptomatic of the new demands of citizenship implicit in the extended commonwealth; while the sense of practical scale, and with it functions, systems, culture, and national societies, almost certainly reflected the spread and growing fiscal cohesiveness of the industrializing sector of the economy in which an older form of wealth was becoming modern capital. "Society," by the nineteenth century, referred to something far more inclusive and locally invasive than any previous ordering of human affairs, something that operated as an agency on its own behalf and that incorporated "individuals" and "groups" through an identification of blood with nation in the privileged juridical form of inherited citizenship. It included for the first time a secular culture, a secular economy, and a secular state.

The discourses in which these terms could be conveniently deployed yielded, by the unavoidable mixing of their fluencies, a variety of concepts: of orderly ensembles such as nation, city, and party; of generalized and infinitely extensible processes like industry and production; of perils of natural or quasi-natural forces such as disaster, the people, the dangerous classes, and riot; and of deliberative agencies that confronted the new citizenry and confirmed in their activities the greater sociological reality of nation beyond the monarch—in the areas of law, the market, and government. These concepts were appropriate to a new culture of space—social and economic rather than as formerly physical or political—and time—dynamic and historical rather than the succession of regimes. For the first time in the West there could be a phenomenology as well as a statics of society, a view of the social as a cohesive order of intentionality with its own development and capacity to regulate the affairs of its "moments" and "instances." The occupation of "intellectual" began to organize itself in regard to this immense community of strangers, the new "society" that confronted nature on its own account and whose maturity would forever after be gauged positively by the integration of proliferating specialties and critically by the problematics of reconciling increasingly generalized differences of purpose.

Social commentary became philosophy and then "science;" and the range of recognizable national differences came to be organized positively as "culture" and subject to those comparisons that would prove fundamental to a later positivist evolutionary anthropology (cf. Burke 1978; Brown 1978). A more subtle and critical philosophy was also inherent in those same discourses, one that elaborated upon the phenomenologically dynamic aspects of society: agency, interest, power, conflict, contradiction, and history (White 1973).

Marx responded to several disciplines within this moral and intellectual ferment, particularly the controversies around the writings of Hegel and the growing expository literature that comprised early economic theory. He was influenced as well by the democratic movements of his century and the emphases in early socialist thought on equality, labor's contribution to social progress, and cooperation (cf. McLellan 1977).

His studies of mathematics gave him access to the mainstream of political economy, but his use of algebra was intended for purposes of exposition rather than analysis per se. Marx's method of exposition required a formal interpretation of certain abstractions, referents deliberately taken out of context (such as the production of commodities), through the algebraic manipulation of propositions. These abstractions were chosen according to two criteria: 1. their centrality to the prevailing uncritical discourses on economy and society that constituted the initial position of Marx's reader and therefore the possibility of critical dialogue; 2. their position in the order of abstractions already established by analytic procedures as sufficient to define the concrete totality of economy and society: that is, the historically specific, self-contradictory and therefore self-transforming ensemble of human affairs that expresses in practice the critical aspect of what had been uncritically asserted to be an operative unity of capitalist production (cf. Brown 1983–84, for a discussion of the methodology of exposition in Marx's *Capital*).

These criteria are apparent in Marx's summary of his critique of political economy at the beginning of volume 3 of *Capital:*

> In Volume I we investigated the phenomena exhibited by the *process of capitalist production,* taken by itself, i.e. the immediate production process, in which connection all secondary influences external to this process were left out of account. But this immediate production process does not exhaust the life cycle of capital. In the world as it actually is, it is supplemented by the *process of circulation,* and this formed our object of investigation in the second volume. Here we showed, particularly in Part Three, where we considered the circulation process as it mediates the process of social reproduction, that the capitalist production process, taken as a whole, is a unity of the production and circulation processes. It cannot be the purpose of the present, third volume simply to make general reflections on this unity. Our concern is rather to discover and present the concrete forms which grow out of the *process of capital's movement considered as a whole.* In their actual movement, capitals confront one another in certain concrete forms, and, in relation to these, both the shape capital assumes in the immediate production process and its shape in the process of circulation appear merely as particular moments. The configurations of capital, as developed in this volume, thus approach step by step the form in which they appear on the surface of society, in the action of different capitals on one another, i.e. in competition, and in the everyday consciousness of the agents of production themselves. [1981b, p. 117; cf. also pp. 966–67]

From this passage it should be clear that for Marx there is a self-transforming interaction, or dialectical relation, of exposition and analysis, though the former begins with the provisionally deconstructed result of analysis and the latter begins with the putative totality of an uncritical theory that fixes on particular abstractions and generalizes as if identifying a totality-defining trend. It should also be clear that what appears to be a succession of stages of development in Marx's exposition (in Volume 1 in particular) is, in the result of analysis, conditions of societal reproduction ordered as more or less general conditions of socioeconomic change and/or social development. The appearance of a narrative (of successive forms of exchange) in Volume 1's exposition of capitalist production should be understood as a feature of that volume's status as abstractive in relation to the completed analysis. Marx's thesis is not that of the unfolding of capitalism through an evolution of primitive production to production mediated by circulation, though it is often presented as that; it is, rather, that of a complex of movements or possible movements in regard to an historically contradictory mode of production.

Marx's use of formal procedures in the exposition of the results of his analysis was not only intended to clarify the implications of abstractions taken by themselves. It was part of the interaction of exposition and analysis by which analysis itself proceeded. Thus, the algebraic manipulation of propositions allowed Marx to clarify the implications and limits of analytically determined abstractions and to demonstrate their dependence for the coherence of argument on further abstractions of "context." Ultimately, this procedure of moving from object to context to the reformulation of the object allowed him to specify the totality whose theoretical concreteness consisted of the ordered set of abstractions by which it could be understood as a self-transformation, an historical process. In this, Marx showed the importance of his debt to Hegel.

Hegel and Marx

Hegel's influence derived from the comprehensiveness of his philosophy and the solution offered by his "phenomenology of mind" to the problem of formulating condition and activity as aspects of the same process. His historical characterization of the distinction between appearance and reality, his identification of subjectivity and objectivity as aspects of a concrete totality whose development had somehow become an issue, and his analysis of the dialectic by which that development could be said to be internal and a materiality of life rather than of inert substance, were basic to Marx's version of "historical materialism." Marx's contribution to dialectics consisted of an interrogation and interpretation of the perspective of totality: he asked how the development of a concrete totality becomes an issue for theory, and he answered in terms of the practical dispersion of general and totalizing interests and the corresponding social relations that define the materiality, or reproducibility, of life and on which would have to be predicated any theoretically valid conception of society as constituted in the activities of people. He accepted the overall logic of Hegel's conception of history in which what can be done depends upon what has been done, every act addresses an unsolvable problem or contradiction within the relations that make action possible, and no act or set of relations can be replicated as such.

Marx rejected the sentimental idealizations of "spirit" and "culture" that had led some of the romantics including, despite himself, Hegel, to glorify the state and elevate its heroic traditions to the level of a *telos*. Instead of an idea of History beyond history, Marx argued that the dialectic of society could only be known within the perspective of a practice and could in no sense be taken to represent eternal laws of nature or humankind. Even the emphasis on production, the core of Marx's materialism, had its validating context: only capital brings people together in a secularizing order of interdependent activities that overcomes the scarcity inherent in fragmented and tradition-oriented practices. Therefore, it is for the critique of capital and capitalism that production stands as the basis of society: production and not culture is the historical achievement of capitalism. Any theory of the latter presupposes a self-historicizing theoretical realization of the former.

This is no doubt why Marx left little indication of what he thought would follow the completion and social transformation of the capitalist revolution. To have done otherwise would have been presumptuously prophetic, would have denied the historical limitations of knowledge with which he began, and would have betrayed the epistemology of his analysis to precisely the sort of speculative fervor that could only discourage the historical imagination (cf., however, Marx 1981b, pp. 288–89, 568, 570–71, 572, 649, 743, 799, 929–30, 986–91; 1981a, pp. 389–93, 500–501; 1976, p. 171).

The shift of emphasis from ideas and ideal unities to practices and social relations implied that progress occurred, if at all, in practical, self-oriented activity and not by the application of principles by subjects removed from historical practice. It also implied that such activity was not simply a rejection of the "status quo." The latter could only be conceived of independently in ideological terms. The choice people had to face was not between accepting things as they were or changing them altogether, but between creating and recreating one thing or another. The "status quo" was itself a constant reconstitution of human affairs, no less so than its practical critique. Marx and Engels gave this a political content when they said in 1848 at the beginning of *The Communist Manifesto*, "the history of all hitherto existing society is the history of class struggles"—which is to say that a total organization of productive effort (and its conceivable antecedents and prospects) is historical in the sense of instituting itself according to an internal dynamic (Marx and Engels 1948). Its political aspect is "class struggle," which, in this formulation, reflects the more fundamental contradictions by which it is possible to conceive of any total organization of production whose social relations are constituted in the development of its economics.

Marx and Classical Economics

Marx's encounter with the classical literature of political economy gave him the language with which to establish the distinctive character of capitalist wealth. Taken as a whole, that literature assumed: 1. that wealth had something to do with what different sorts of products had in common; 2. that this commonality could be measured and its variation made a direct object of policy; 3. that it was somehow embodied in all objects that could be sold, bought, and used; 4. and that both the exchangeability and utility of such objects were consistent features of their objectivity.

The first two assumptions were necessary to explain the ratio of exchange among goods, a fundamental problem of early economics. The third accounted for the composition of wealth, and the fourth provided the image of a rational connection between the generalized production of goods and the universal market in which, theoretically, goods were sold such that sales could give rise to further production. The application of these assumptions to the "real" economy of production and exchange required an answer to the question: what made goods valuable? and the further question: what bearing did the value of goods have on decisions to produce them?

For Adam Smith and the "classical economists," the value of goods depended upon the labor employed in their production. "Labor" referred to the sum of concrete productive activities, an inventory of tasks analyzed as costs. It followed that the value of a good equalled the costs that it realized upon sale. But if this were all, there would be no reason for anyone to continue production. The realization of one's costs is not an incentive to engage in productive activity. Yet, people produced and goods were exchanged. The price of goods had then to depend upon something other than their costs, and therefore on something outside of production altogether. This led some economists to claim that the value of a good depended upon the market and therefore its manifest ratio of exchange with other goods. But to explain value (of produced goods) by price (sold goods) was to beg the question that had led to the need for a theory of value in the first place: how to explain the ratio of exchange so as to account for a continual stimulus to production. An ad hoc formula was introduced to avoid the problem: in the vastness of the market lay opportunities unevenly distributed. Those in a position to take advantage of them would profit and the profitability of the sector so developed would attract other investors until that market sector was saturated and new alternative opportunities emerged. But while the unevenness of the market may be a fact, it is still something that needs to be explained. Without that explanation, no analysis is possible of the accumulation of wealth and the rational composition of an economy.

One alternative to reversing cause and effect, value and price, was to explain prices, and presumably wealth and production, by a theory of consumption. The value of a good would, on this account, depend upon its usefulness to buyers. But what is useful cannot easily be determined in advance and may indeed be arbitrary. Therefore the theory was inconsistent with the requirement that value be measurable. Without the possibility of measurement, there could be no analysis of the relationship between the composition of wealth and production.

The failure of classical economics was nevertheless tempered by its emphasis on labor, and in Smith's discussion Marx found the kernel of a solution to the problem of value. The solution required a shift from the idea of value as a quality embodied in particular goods to value as a quality of commodities in relation to one another as commodities, including their relation to what Marx was to show to be the commodity "labor power."[1]

The "labor theory of value" became, in Marx's hands, a sociological conception in which society was identified by the relationship between its most general product and its most general form of competence to that product:

> The general form of value, . . . can only arise as the joint contribution of the whole world of commodities. A commodity only acquires a general expression of its value if, at the same time, all other commodities express their values in the same equivalent; . . . It thus becomes evident that because the objectivity of commodities as values is the purely "social existence" of these things, it can only be expressed through the whole range of their social relations; consequently the form of their value must possess social validity. . . . In this manner the labour objectified in the values of commodities is not just presented negatively, as labour in which abstraction is made from all the concrete forms and useful properties of actual work. Its own positive nature is explicitly brought out, namely the fact that it is the reduction of all kinds of actual labour to their common character of being human labour in general, of being the expenditure of human labour-power. . . . In this way it is made plain that within this world [of commodities] the general human character of labour forms its specific social character. [Marx 1976, pp. 159–160].

For critical economics Marx's theory of value showed that the relationship between production and the circulation of capital (as goods or money) was self-transforming, interactive in the dialectical sense, and *therefore incapable of structural rationalization*. For the sociological imagination, it showed that the value of any good depended upon the fact that its production amounted to *the extraction of a portion of productive power from society and its diversion to one use instead of another*. This will be clarified in later chapters. For now, it should be easy to see why the fate of sociology would, from the publication of Marx's writings, be tied to political economy, and why the established discipline of economics had to elide the historical implications and therefore the substance of the labor theory of value.

Not all of the evasion can be traced, however, to class bias. There are four additional reasons why the dependence of capital on labor was difficult to perceive. First, parties are normally consumed by the particular transactions in which they are involved. The immediacy of work or exchange tends to make obscure the wider contexts and the historical dynamic upon which they depend. Context and history become apparent only when capitalist economy so dominates productive activity and the distribution of goods that extra-local considerations are impossible to avoid.

But even then, and this is the second reason, the forms in which transactions take place may disguise their actual content. The wage contract gives the appearance of freedom, fairness, and equality. Each party seems to make a promise and to enter into a legal relationship voluntarily. The wage itself, a payment of money for time spent at work, seems to involve an exchange of equal values, though we have already seen that it cannot be: labor must create more than it costs to employ if production is to provide incentives for capital. Third, the very employment of money as the currency against which all goods and services are exchanged seems to belie the contribution of labor and the primacy of production. Finally, the legal enforcement of property rights, the obligations of contract, and adherence to the strictures of the market suggest a ratification of the primacy of property by at least tradition if not nature or morality.

The fact that production could only occur if there were an incentive to produce, given that incentive depends upon profitability, which in turn reflects the capacity of labor to produce more than its own cost, led Marx to interpret workers' protests, whatever their immediate content, as attempts to reclaim the surplus value that labor created and capital expropriated, and, correspondingly, to interpret official responses to protest as manifesting two policies: 1. the attempt to legitimize state control of the working class through legislation against "combination," the use of military force in labor disputes, and the establishment of various organizational means to protect private property; and 2. the development of ideologies disguised as theories, moral and scientific, that justified state action even beyond its claim to represent the "common good."

The social sciences incorporated these ideologies in the form of a general distinction between rational action (governed by considerations of exchange and respect for property) and irrational behavior (that interfered with the prescribed detachment of exchange from needs and affections and therefore with those prerogatives of property that were inconsistent with collective needs). This distinction was discursively substantiated by reference to riot, the dangerous classes, mass behavior, mob violence, and communism (cf. Wolfe 1973; Brown 1979a; Brown and Goldin 1973), and supported theories of "collective" and "mass" behavior consistent with the most antidemocratic tendencies of capitalist economy (cf. Brown and Goldin 1973, for a review). The use of those theories to justify policies of social control at the end of the nineteenth century was one of the first intellectual expressions of anticommunist ideology. Ironically, they also provided, through their elevation of the metaphors of "crowd," "mob," and "mass" to the status of ideas, one crucial rationale for the establishment of academic sociology in the United States.

This dual evasion, at once practical and theoretical, has been discussed by contemporary theorists of the state, and in socially critical historical research that demonstrates the deliberative, organized, and political aspects of working class and popular movements (cf., for example, Rudé 1964; Hobsbawm 1973; Samuel 1981; Thompson 1963). The critique of political economy led through those literatures to a political sociology more appropriate to the Marxian tradition than to the antihistorical and administrative theories of organization that had inherited the discipline of sociology after its establishment in the academy. By the last third of the twentieth century, this new political sociology was able to deal simultaneously with the inherent crises of capitalist institutions—such as the state, education, and the media— and organized protest (cf. Miliband 1969, 1977; Poulantzas 1973, 1975; Aronowitz 1973; Bowles and Gintis 1976; Ewen 1976; Parenti 1985; O'Connor 1973; Habermas 1975; cf. Kesselman 1982; Flacks and Turkel 1978).

The dialectical conception of history and the economists' reluctant acknowledgement of labor's significance for the meaning as well as accumulation of wealth gave Marx the intellectual means with which to identify the significant dimensions of capitalist production. From these he would conclude that the capitalist mode of production was a way of producing an increasing number of goods that emerged in a context of precapitalist scarcity. Early commerce had enabled those who had already acquired more immediately tangible forms of wealth than capitalism would eventually recognize to gain control over some of the conditions of production. But it was not until the discovery of the tremendous productive power inherent in combinations of workers—in advanced manufacture and the factory—that the market could be made virtually rational and independent and its currency supply a standard by which factors of production (including labor) could be compared directly with goods. The old wealth in fixed property, title, rare materials, and force gave way under those circumstances to the new wealth, expandable units of capital realized as money profit. The old wealth, the result of direct expropriations, became a new wealth whose production represented the progressive universalization of exploitation.

The juxtaposition of the money market and productive exploitation provided the impulse necessary for a total transformation of social life; but their generalized imposition, what would eventually be called "institutionalization," uprooted populations, destroyed traditions, shattered the continuity of generations and with it family and community, and created a new dialectic of freedom and bondage. What remained was capitalist production, the circulation of goods and people on a market indifferent to distinctions of quality and need, and a new society that, for all its apparent durability, was subject to fundamental contradictions and therefore historical through and through.

Marx and Socialism

All of this followed Marx's use of the dialectic and the rigor with which he reformulated and extended the labor theory of value. The relevance of his theory to practice, and therefore its own confirmation as part of the history it identified, depended upon Marx's appreciation of the significance of a growing opposition that had already articulated itself in terms of its class component, and his demonstration that such an opposition was inevitable within the capitalist mode of production. This theme of class struggle is constant in the Marxian tradition, from the early writings of Marx and Engels through Marx's mature formulation in *Capital* to current political economy. Early socialist thought reinforced this theme in Marx's writings, independently of the philosophical debates about history and the relation of theory to practice.

The early socialists provided a vision of a nonexploitive, cooperative society that represented what within democratic theory responded to the dilemmas of competitive individualism by formulating and enacting the idea of a collective agency prior to individuals, informed by an innate spirit of cooperation. Despite its obvious appeal, and the occasional experiments in England and the United States that made it seem feasible, socialism in the first half of the nineteenth century was unable to show how it could achieve universality, particularly in the historical context of an expanding capitalism. For Marx, this historical impracticality marked it as utopian, but not necessarily idealistic. Its vision was grounded in the productive nature of the society to which it responded—one founded in fact upon the possibility of cooperative labor on an unlimited scale. Despite the religiosity that often informed its expressions, socialism corresponded to the moral demands of a secularization that could henceforth never peaceably be undone. It reflected, though without steady articulation, the paradox that even capitalists found hard to ignore—that the social production of wealth ultimately required at least some degree of restrictive social control over legally recognized private property.

Marx replaced the utopianism with an historical analysis of the way in which socialism becomes necessary within the capitalist mode of production itself and the conditions under which it could be, to any degree, realized—conditions that would vary with the development of capital. By "socialism" he meant not only an economy without exploitive relations of production but one in which society would control rather than be controlled by its wealth. Its elements were already present in capitalism as the socialization of production and the productive collectivization of work. An interest in sustaining the productivity of the capitalist mode of production as a whole was therefore, by definition, a socialist interest. Given the historical limitations of the capitalist mode of production, as well as its accomplishment, that could be the only rationally derived universal interest; it was also, by analysis, labor's interest.

Labor, organized under capitalism as the "society of the producers," made socialism possible; private ownership of the means of production, a principle hostile to its own status and capability, made it necessary. By showing that capitalism depended upon the society of producers that capital could not tolerate as a society, Marx situated the socialist vision in the world of practice and the latter in the midst of class struggle—that is, in the context of capitalism itself.

Marxism and Capitalism

The fact that the Marxian critique of capital attempts to grasp the capitalist mode of production as a whole requires further attention to an issue of methodology that was discussed in chapter 2. No one and no theory can directly grasp a total arrangement of life's activities. It can only be grasped through concepts that make sense of experience beyond its particularities. But since theory attempts to challenge what we think we know rather than to provide knowledge through discoveries made independently of what we think we know, it can only begin as the critique of prevailing conceptualizations (cf. Sartre 1976; Althusser 1970; Brown 1983–84). Theoretical work is itself a dialectic of criticism and self-criticism, a movement through the temptations of prevailing formulae rather than merely against them.

Marxian analysis begins then as a critical investigation of prevailing concepts of economy, politics, and society. It attempts to clarify the problematic character of the unity of objects presumed by the anticritical use of referential terms. It does not deny the importance of examining the logical ordering of propositions or of accumulating data, but employs these as subsidiary techniques to the main lines of critical methodology.

Marx found the most explicit and well-established concepts in the writings of the economists where they were used to justify the privacy of property and the productive superiority of capital to labor. As we will see, the putative unities of commodity, capital, labor, and market disguised paradoxes inherent in the practices associated with them. A commodity was an object with a price. It was also an object of use. Its production had to be justified both in terms of its capacity to circulate, to be exchanged for money, and in terms of its suitability to needs. But the first cannot guarantee the second, and the second resists a money translation.

Similarly, "capital" referred to both profit and means of production; but what is profitable to produce may and often does deplete the general store of resources necessary for production. "Labor" was at once the act of creating something and a cost calculated against profit; but the calculation of cost must be indifferent to the concrete activity of creating concrete items or it will lose its capacity to refer to the mobility of employment and wage that enhances the profitability of investment. "Market" referred to both the circulation of money and the circulation of value as capital; but while money may be a token of value, the two vary independently, though within limits. The assertion of a unity in each case denied a more fundamental disunity.

Marx's critique provided a better account of capitalism than that of the economists in several respects: 1. His theory was established on the basis of a critique of concepts already in use that transformed their meaning rather than attempted to displace them immediately and altogether; 2. His critique of political economy demonstrated that the unities asserted in conventional formulations were inconsistent with their practical and historical implications; 3. It showed as well that its results, particularly in regard to the importance of socialized labor, were presupposed but yet suppressed in standard accounts; 4. His theory encompassed the history and not merely the form or apparent structure of capitalism, thereby avoiding illusions of stability and permanence in favor of conflict and the irrepressibility of social change.

Note

1. "The linen, by virtue of the form of value, no longer stands in a social relation with merely one other kind of commodity, but with the whole world of commodities as well. As a commodity it is a citizen of that world" (Marx 1976, p. 155).

5

Labor's Capitalism and Capitalist Society

THE FOLLOWING VERSION of Marxian theory is aimed at providing a foundation for social theory in a sociological interpretation of the labor theory of value: *the value of a product expresses the difference it makes to the society that produces it.*

We begin with four working hypotheses: (1) the overwhelming domination of capitalist society by its economy is apparent in the character of the production and use of an historically distinctive kind of wealth; (2) that domination is inherently ambiguous in its practical expression and discursive realization; (3) the uniqueness and extreme effects of this ambiguity can be understood in terms of the logic of capitalist production as a whole, but only indicated by the empirical division of populations by classes; (4) class conflict is sufficiently well-documented that the perspectives of either capital or labor provide immediately plausible alternative conceptualizations of society independently of their theoretical justification.

Marxian theory recognizes the validity of both the experience of property and the experience of work. The former provides the initial movement of theoretical exposition in part because it is the immediate operating principle of capitalist production, the focus of prevailing theories, the central concern of policymakers, and the governing metaphor of the ideological imagination of the capitalist class. That it is superceded in the dialectic of Marxian theory by the perspective of labor is due to its own limitations. These are established in the critical demonstration that the maintenance of property as capital depends upon an expanding socialization of labor, and that capital cannot on its own account project the sort of universal interest necessary for the practical realization of the society it needs.

Thus, Marx begins *Capital* by examining products independently of the processes by which they are created. He begins with the abstract "commodity" and the discourse in which the term is conveniently used. He notes, on the first pages of Volume 1 of *Capital,* that it is commonly thought that the society of capitalist production depends upon the wealth that accumulates under its national banner and that this wealth consists of precisely what it appears to, namely goods. But it is not clear whether goods are produced because they are intended to serve the needs of people or because they can be exchanged for a monetary profit. The analogy of the free barter in which one useful thing is traded for another, thereby satisfying the needs of all the trading parties, suggests the former; the analogy of the free market, with its circulation of goods and money without regard to substance suggests the latter.

Barter is an exchange of useful goods between individuals to their immediate mutual benefit. It presupposes a compatibility of needs whose satisfaction is the purpose of productive activity and the standard by which any exchange is evaluated. The idea of the money market is that of a virtual nature that operates on its own account, independently of intentions and concerns and to which all individual transactions must ultimately pay their due. It presupposes that a productive activity will continue if and only if someone is willing and able to pay money for its products and the return on sales is sufficient to realize costs.

Since this relatively "free" market depends upon steady supplies of saleable goods, every good produced—if it is not to drain productive capacity—must be comparable to and therefore exchangeable for every other. Moreover, the important and most easily recognized beneficiary of trade is the seller. On this account, needs are of no particular economic significance, and the work of producing something distinct is less important than the work of selling it for a price that measures what it has in common with other goods, including those that serve as productive facilities. The particular product and its distinctive qualities need have no intrinsic appeal and are in principle irrelevant to its salability. On the strength of the analogy of the market, rational economic activity must refer to something other than needs or processes of production. On the strength of the analogy of barter, neither production nor exchange on a scale greater than the interpersonal transaction can provide a basis for an economy.

The analogies of barter and free market typically serve different ideological purposes. Clearly, they are entirely too abstract to serve the purposes of theory. Barter suggests a democratic justification for capitalist economy: the servicing of needs and the absolute freedom and equality of exchange. The market's justification is explicitly hostile to democracy in favor of privilege: it suggests that privileges have been earned, that the strength of a society lies in its capacity to reward those who are dogged and clever, and that the freedom to buy and sell must be given absolute priority if there is to be an overall order to production and a socially valid integration of the innate selfishness of human beings.

When they appear together as they often do, "barter" typically justifies and "market" is used to explain the profit-oriented economy. But the incompatibility of the justification and explanation, the reason and the process, invites scrutiny. Capitalism cannot be justified by the useful things it provides and explained by the operations of a market that is indifferent to needs. Nor, it follows, can capitalism be defined as a system of producing useful items for sale and the wealth of capitalist society as the sum of such items.

In order to maintain two contradictory positions, it is necessary to ignore whatever makes the contradiction explicit. To justify capitalism in terms of barter, it is necessary to ignore the scale of capitalist economy and the ways in which that scale separates interpersonal transactions and economic processes independent of individuals. To explain it in terms of the free market, one must ignore differences of opportunity and, above all, the contribution of labor. Similarly, to account for the value of goods by their putative usefulness ignores the fact that they are made to be sold, and to explain it in terms of their marketability is to deny that they are made to be used (Marx, 1976, chap 1).

The evasion of this contradiction led to a sectoral economics of the market and a theory of prices that suspended altogether any obligation to account for the capitalist economy as a whole, while barter became one of the key metaphors for the primitivist sociology of the nineteenth century social evolutionists and one formula for justifying the liberal theory of laissez faire. In each case, the idealization that was left intact by the evasion of inconsistency marked those conceptualizations as ideological. But it was only possible to move beyond this critique by exploring the implications of the most fundamental propositions available to the economics of capital. In this regard, Marx emphasized the nature of the commodity as an historically specific form of product and attempted to show that the social aspects of production taken as a whole are its constitutive features.

Is the commodity a "simple thing" whose value depends upon both its capacity to satisfy peoples' needs and its price? If one, what of the other and if both, how are they to be reconciled? Is wealth the sum of useful goods? Is the market something on the order of an ecology controlling the fates of its regions? The discourses of vast scale and the exchange of quantities provided the intellectual tools for the analysis of modern economy in the nineteenth century. Marx, therefore, began by examining the idea of the market, the universal exchangeability of goods, and concluded by showing that it implies a socially rational process of production that its practice can neither facilitate nor guarantee.

The following sections summarize the course of this analysis, beginning with a discussion of the most general form in which a product is recognizable as a marketable good, the commodity. Following is an examination of the concepts of labor, value, and labor power, each of which will be discussed in connection with basic concepts in sociology.

Commodities

A commodity is anything that is produced exclusively in order to be sold. But goods can only be sold if there are people willing and able to buy them; and that will depend upon, among other things, how the price of any good compares with the prices of similar but competing goods. Later, we will see that the production of a good for sale depends on its capacity to realize a greater value than is required for its production.

It follows that in general the choice of what to produce and how to produce it cannot reasonably depend upon attitudes toward craft, task, or materials. Similarly, the activity of selling cannot depend upon the extra-economic relations of buyer and seller (relative status, kinship, obligations of membership in a community, and the like), judgments about the buyer's needs, or considerations of sympathy, fairness, or loyalty; nor can it depend upon moral, aesthetic, or noneconomic practical evaluations of any sort about any object, person, or condition. That all of these do enter economic transactions merely indicates the contradictory relation of economy to society. The success of profitable enterprise requires an antisocial mixture of indifference, calculation, and an impersonal and insatiable interest in the expansion of fortune. It is therefore inconsistent with the idea that goods are produced either to serve society or to serve the needs of people, and with the related idea that the work of producing a good could be precious for its own pleasurable qualities such as craft, profession, and/or contribution to society.

The usefulness of a good is only formally relevant to the decision to produce it: it is measured strictly by the likelihood that it will in fact be purchased, not whether it will be consumed. It is clear then that without monopolistic control the most important human needs—food, shelter, education, comfort, medical care, and the like—are not easily manipulated and, in any case, are insufficiently flexible to be a basis for profitable enterprise. They are satisfied if at all in familiar ways and by conservative standards: one can only eat so much. In fact, any good that people routinely purchase tends to lead to self-regulation or regulation by local and/or induced norms and therefore to limitations on purchasing. The markets for such goods are rapidly saturated so that their sale cannot provide sufficient incentive to guarantee their continual production.

There is a difference between being motivated by a need and being motivated to buy regardless of one's needs. When our needs are satisfied, we no longer wish to buy; we relax and go about our affairs. On the other hand, buying without reference to need is an activity like panic or play: it feeds on itself. The act of purchasing is deeply socialized. It responds to images and representations that reflect a received priority of things over people (cf. Ewen 1976). To the extent to which it is not grounded in needs appropriate to a collective practice, it is at best subject to external manipulation.

To act in a way that bears on the satisfaction of one's need is to learn something about ones self; to act in a way that is indifferent to need is to reproduce only those principles implicit in acts that have no reference to needs, most significantly the principle of manipulation. A capitalist economy would be stifled if it were devoted to the satisfaction of needs; its ideology would fail if it were to acknowledge the legitimacy of needs. Indeed, the very expression of need is an obstacle to capitalist production, not its stimulus or occasion.

It is nevertheless true that capitalist production depends exclusively upon the fact that goods can be sold. Yet, there is no doubt that they can only be sold if they can be referred to some other purpose than trade. Otherwise, purchase is unaccountable to sale. We have already seen that this other purpose, whatever it is and though we still may call it "use," has nothing in particular to do with the concrete uses of things to satisfy peoples' needs. The usefulness of goods, without which their purchase as an act of choice is incomprehensible, must lie in something other than the actual possibility of their use. In other words, the meaning of "usefulness," so far as it refers to commodities, must be different from what it appeared to be in the original justification of capitalist production. It can pertain neither to distinguishing qualities of commodities nor individually specifiable needs.[1]

It follows that a capitalist economy neither requires nor supports a theory of consumption, but only a theory of demand that rigorously excludes reference to needs and satisfactions. What appears to be a paradox is the point of departure both for capital's theory of enterprise and the Marxian critique of that theory. Both must agree that capitalist production is indifferent to human need. But this is why for capital the market is economically decisive whereas for Marxian theory the indifference is the initial point of critique. While capital's economist wishes to, but cannot, show that the free market ultimately provides the greatest satisfaction for the greatest number, thereby justifying a separation of the "politics" of "distribution" from the "economics" of "production," the Marxian theorist explores the implications of the socially ungoverned market's incompatibility with its human subjects, taken singly and as a society. While capital's economist stops at the point at which argument satisfies the motive for profit, Marxian analysis continues to the point at which it discloses the relationship of the market to people as part of an historical play of interests—something to be worked out rather than merely rationalized.

"Usefulness," in the context of the capitalist market, refers to the relation of the product to behavior rather than to need, to the likelihood of, rather than the reason for, its purchase. "Demand" replaces "need" in the lexicon of metaeconomics as an abstraction that dissolves all differences of purpose, reason and value; and theories of social stratificaton correspondingly recognize no scale of difference but that of ability to purchase. This version of "usefulness" makes no reference to whether the market includes starving or otherwise destitute families, concerned parents, unemployed workers, the medically needy, committed scholars or activists, gadget-hungry suburbanites, speculators, or the rich; nor can it refer to collective needs for education, housing, transportation, and security. This rigorous indifference to the human component of the market is of the essence of capitalist economy and all that is rational in its terms. It should be noted that the rejection of "use-value" as a criterion for investment and production helps explain one of the more devastating contradictions of capitalism, namely its inability to guide production sufficiently to provide even the proliferation of capital goods upon which it depends. It is not just that the capitalist mode of production cannot provide for people, it cannot provide adequate conditions for its own technical stability (Marx 1981a, cf. chap. 20, 21).

MONEY

The economic value of products to capital has nothing to do with their actual capacity to serve people's needs but with their relative positions among the various commodities available on the market, and therefore the ratio of their exchange with other things. Since money is the standard by which that ratio is computed in particular transactions, money itself appears to be the source of value and the market the determinant of differences in the value of goods (cf. Marx 1976, chap. 3; and cf. 1981a, pt. 1, chap. 18).

We are far from the "democratic" conceptions of economy that relate production to people or to society. What we have instead seems to be an economics restricted to the immediate and calculable situation of abstracted buyers and sellers, and one that depends solely upon the exchange of things that vary in amount but not quality. The emphasis by capital's economist on exchange and the exchangeability of commodities as the source of value is an improvement in consistency over the idealization of value as an expression of the usefulness of things to people. It emphasizes the accumulative aspect of capitalist wealth and its dominance over the economy of that wealth's production. But it is still a onesided perspective that assumes a society of producers that capitalism must not acknowledge but cannot do without.[2] To support this conclusion it is necessary to look more closely at the idea of money itself within the context of capitalist economy.

Marx points out that money cannot be something that stands above the world of commodities if it is to account for their value. It that were so, one would have to explain money in other than economic terms and the money market would then appear to be a device imposed upon rather than an institution of the economy. On the contrary, money must be something on the same order as the commodities whose value it determines, since if it were not, it could not be both an object of exchange and a standard. It is fair to say then that money is a commodity, though one with special properties. In order to describe it in these terms, it is necessary to review its primary function and the operative "structure" that assigns that function to a commodity rather than to something else.

Ideally, anyone who produces a good for sale will attach a money price to it that compares favorably with the prices of other similar and equally accessible goods; and anyone who buys will buy according to such a comparison. Obviously, not everyone has sufficient information to buy or sell rationally; nor is everyone in a position to take advantage of whatever information they may have. But, assuming that they are not financially impregnable, people can only survive as buyers and sellers if they operate in this way. Even the market as a whole can only continue to function if comparisons among goods are generally possible and if people generally act on them, at least in principle.

If there were no such things as coins, bills, and notes, the regular exchange of goods would still standardize itself: one good would eventually become the standard by which all others could be compared. Otherwise, there could be no extensive exchange, no reliability in trade, no way of gauging the satisfaction of debts, and no market beyond that of simple barter or the futility of exchanging goods for promises of an incalculable return. Coins and bills are substitutes for this "universal commodity" and represent the possibility of evaluating every good in terms of every other. Their use expresses relations among centers of production. As tangible means of exchange, they articulate different standards so that people can trade across production boundaries.

"Money" is the word we use to refer to the specific form that the universal commodity must take in the capitalist market. From the standpoint of theory, the money form is the standard of exchange. From the standpoint of the practical reality to which the theory refers, it is necessary to identify the tangible object that for a variety of reasons in a given society has come to represent the money form. Marx argued that the extensive exchange of goods (and therefore the possibility of their production for the purpose of exchange) requires a standard object that is itself produced and to which all others can be compared, one that is uniform and divisible in its empirical qualities, and that has value as well as allows value to be determined for the practice of exchange. Gold and certain other precious metals have precisely those properties. When minted as coins of different denominations (even when represented by paper), they provide a clear and unambiguous measure that can be used to account for every legitimate economic activity (Marx 1976, chap 3).

As we will see, it does not follow from this that the general level of prices or ratios of exchange among commodities on the market will be coordinated with the costs of producing key goods, capable of realizing the value used up in production, or able to account for the further expansion of productive capacity. To appreciate this paradox, the contradiction of price and value, it is necessary to recall that actual coins, bills, and notes are merely tokens of something more fundamental. They represent the fact that the market requires any good to be exchangeable for any other. The idea of a "universal commodity" represented by dollars, francs, or pounds, is necessary if we are to talk about the production of goods for sale rather than, as in a barter "economy," for immediate use.

But even this "universal commodity" is not the basis of capitalist exchange. It reflects what would go on in the market if it were described as separate from production, but does not explain the market itself. It accounts for how commodities relate to each other, but not how they get to be commodities that can have a standard form and, in terms of that form, interact through the vehicle of exchange. It is apparent that the idealized, independently rational order of the market, registered as the flow of goods and money, actually depends on a steady and uninterrupted supply of goods and on some way of making sure that the supply serves the precise needs of production (equipment, transportation facilities, and so on) and the needs of the social forms in which production is carried out—domestic facilities that prepare the worker to work, social arrangements to insure that people at a distance from one another can rely on a certain mutality of effort, and the sorts of consumer goods that nourish, protect, and secure the individuals and groups that make up the "society of the producers" (Marx 1981b, p. 358). It is also apparent that all of these goods contribute to the marketability of goods in general if and only if their sale (in general) contributes to the order of production. Without that contribution, without the order of production, there are no commodities and hence there is no market. The universal standardizing market must, then, nourish whatever makes it possible. This is obviously labor; but it is labor conceived of as the "society of producers," whose capacity to produce is to some extent determined by standards of work and living established independently of the imperatives of the capitalist accumulation of wealth:

> The *true barrier* to capitalist production is *capital itself*. It is that capital and its self-valorization appear as the starting and finishing point, as the motive and purpose of production; production is production only for *capital*, and not the reverse, i.e. the means of production are not simply means for a steadily expanding pattern of life for the *society* of the producers [Marx 1981b, p. 358].

It is that society of producers that fully institutes labor as a class and constitutes its class interest as social in the strictest sense of the term.

For anyone buying or selling in a particular situation at a particular time, or for anyone who cares to look at such local transactions as the sole index of economy, money will appear to be the overwhelming reality and the proper object of analysis. When we look at the economy as a whole, in terms of its social relations, it is clear that money itself depends upon the more fundamental fact of labor, but only if "labor" means more than the simple performance of a task or the steady performance of an "occupation."

Before enlarging upon this in regard to the discussion so far, it is necessary to review what has become of the concepts "wealth" and "commodity." From something originally thought to be essentially useful, the commodity now appears to be an object produced for sale regardless of whether or not it can be used to satisfy needs. From this point of view, its salient characteristic is its price, and prices are determined by the operation of a market that assumes steady, continually expanding, and socially rational production. For various reasons, these assumptions cannot be sustained in practice: the tokens used to calculate price may cease to correspond to the value (societal facilities) consumed in production; the use of profit by private parties for their own benefit cannot guarantee a rational reinvestment of the surplus in the facilities that make social production (and its profits) possible. The reality of production makes itself felt at all times even as its disregard by the market constantly threatens it. Even in its onesided identification as capital's unique social product, the commodity is either an unrealizable form or a practical indication of a contradition in the division of production.

Similarly, society's wealth was initially characterized as the sum of its useful goods. However, the fact that goods are produced by a society of producers but exclusively for a sale that benefits those who stand apart from and in opposition to that society implies paradoxically either that there is no wealth that can properly be called society's or that the wealth of capital is not the sort of wealth that can contribute to society's continued existence as a productive agency. In other words, it now appears that "wealth" refers to the accumulated capacity of society to produce; but that this social capacity is privately owned and employed for the benefit of its owners suggests that the term "society" refers either to the competitive and therefore asocially anarchistic combination of owners or to an economically mobilized population that lacks the capacity to organize itself. Neither is what is typically meant by "society." What was originally thought to be society's wealth or the "wealth of the nation" is, at most, an index of a feature of the market as such: capitalist wealth must circulate if it is to account for the capacity of capital to provide for its own continued expansion; it must have a fluidity that has no extra-economic societal qualification whatsoever. *But then it cannot be the wealth of society.*

It is of course true that capital created its *labor force* by bringing people together in massive territories of work. But the essential sociality of that force, the conditions of interaction and mutual support, the practices by which people come to know themselves as members of a community of workers and a society of producers, cannot be, nor have been, provided by any deliberately rational act of capital, since the cost of that sociality necessarily detracts from the free circulation of goods upon which the profits of capital depend. Therefore, *the society of producers,* society as such, the society for which wealth is an historical problem, must have been created by and be maintained in the acts of the producing population itself. This is the history of labor as a class against the history of its class antagonist, capital. And, as will be shown, this antagonism, so apparent in the overall movements of the political economy, derives from the fundamental and interior division of production into the mutually necessary yet incompatible operations of labor and capital.

So far, this investigation points to the conclusion that a fully developed capitalist economy does not and cannot produce what people need if they are to work and live together as workers. Therefore it cannot serve society as such beyond providing a formally adequate basis of production for a societal order barely recognizable and yet to be fully instituted. It suggests, as well, that whatever social order exists does so within the society of producers and is created by them on behalf of but incompatibly with the profit economy of capital. It also suggests that attempts by that society to assert its needs will be answered by any available means necessary to ensure the continued circulation of capitalist wealth and its principle of control by private parties for their own benefit: the movement of production facilities to places where such demands can be effectively ignored, the attempt to institute political or fiscal constraints on the expression of social demands, the institution of ideological devices intended to make the basis of social demands hopelessly obscure, the use of force and even war—anything that seems likely to preserve that "freedom of enterprise" that cannot endure the freedom and democracy of "society."

On the other hand, since the operations of the market depend upon production, it is clear that in one way or another and despite the immediate interests of individual capitalists and the inability of the capitalist economy as a whole to combine those interests in a class-protective *or* socially rational policy, that dependence will have its historical effects. From Marx's point of view the question is not so much how production affects the market as the nature of the problem and how fractions of capital and labor accommodate to it.

The result for his analysis was the development of a series of "best" cases, an exploration of possible evolutions of capitalist accumulation seen as attempts to deal with crises at each stage that are, successively, internal to accumulation itself, a result of the contradiction of the market with the society of producers, a reflection of the pressure of value (the needs of social production) on price, and connected with the development of the special sociality by which the society of producers becomes conscious of its interest as society and demonstrates degrees of that consciousness in various types of collective demand and class conflict (cf. Marx 1976, app.).[3]

Thus, the relationships that become apparent through the Marxian critique of capital are, in some sense, idealized—not that they are unreal but that they represent the most rational courses capital can take, the most rational version of the development of the capitalist division of labor for capital, given the fundamental historical dynamic of the capitalist mode of production. This is at the same time the strongest case for the contradictory character of capitalist economy, for its ultimate inability to provide for its own continuation, precisely because the analysis takes seriously the point of view of capital. That is to say, Marx provided a "critique of capital" aimed at showing its own paradoxical nature, the crises that it cannot despite its best efforts avoid, and the conflict that it constantly attempts but must fail to manage.[4]

Labor and Value

Given the theoretical priority of difference, opposition, and contradiction, it is necessary to discuss more fully the relations of value, price, and labor in order to establish for capital's *best cases* the value-related parameters of the circulation of money, goods, and people. Marx was led in this regard to a factor often mentioned in passing but never realized in conventional theory: the underlying source of value, what ensured accountable relationships between every productive act and the market, and every instance of exchange and the general order of production, was that whatever its price, quality, or use, each commodity was a product of socially organized human labor.

Appearances to the contrary, Marx demonstrated that the value of commodities does not depend exclusively upon the sum of the immediate costs of their production (Marx, 1981, chs. 8 and 9). Their price may reflect such costs to some extent, but the factors that contribute to those costs are diverse and cannot be added to one another. Some costs pertain to things—equipment, plant, material—and some to people—labor. Capital can realize the cost of things, but it profits only from the use of labor.

Equipment and plant are costs, but they do not themselves account for profitable enterprise. The price of a good reflects a portion of the cost of equipment, plant, and material, but what the capitalist gets from selling the goods, so far as those factors are concerned, is merely a return on the cost of maintaining them (and depreciation). This may be passed on to the consumer, but if the price is artificially inflated to yield a greater profit than could be accounted for by those costs, the price will cease to be competitive and people will buy from someone else. The capitalist cannot ask the machinery to do more than it was designed to do or to live a less satisfying life in order to work harder or for longer hours. It must be maintained in good working order if it is to retain its capacity, and its capacity is limited by its design. Therefore, the rational seller within a given industry can only include as that part of the selling price of a good that corresponds to equipment, plant, and material the portion of their value that is immediately used in a given period of production. Any more would be an arbitrary charge that competitors would not have to match.

These factors cannot, by themselves, produce; nor can they account for the profitability of enterprise without which capital would not have organized production in the first place. Human labor is something altogether different. It can make do with changing circumstances. Therefore, its cost can vary in ways that the cost of machines cannot. Labor can produce more than is needed to maintain it and it can be redesigned and redirected without increasing its cost.

Labor is the significant factor in the production of capitalist wealth because human effort can vary along a wide range, people can produce more in concert than they can as individuals, and even as individuals they can produce more than they need to survive and continue working. Capitalist wealth is represented by money; but it corresponds to a quantitatively variable surplus of product beyond the cost of labor. This surplus, represented by salable goods, is its ultimate content. Labor is economically significant in the capitalist mode of production only to the extent to which it contributes to the profit of capital that corresponds to the surplus product (Marx 1976, 1038–49). This surplus is significant only to the extent to which it can be used to expand capital's control over production through the application to production itself of the monetary token of the surplus that comes to capital by way of sales of commodities (cf. Marx 1976, pp. 131–54).

This is, as we have seen, valid in the sense that it is the best case for capital to rationalize production in its own interest. The economic significance of labor for *society,* however, lies in its production of surplus *value;* not simply more goods but goods that directly contribute to the productivity of society. The capitalist evaluates labor as his or her cost of production, beyond the inert factors: labor represents no more than an outlay of money (the wage) relative to the capitalist's income; and, holding speculation constant, the surplus provided by that labor (what is produced beyond what is necessary to account for the cost of labor itself) is considered to be an amount of goods represented primarily by their price above the price of the wage (Marx 1978, chap. 10).

Because of the relative independence of enterprises, the capitalist sees value (the significance of a product to society) in terms of price.[5] Because of the exigencies of the immediate situation in which he or she operates (including competition), the capitalist must lower the wage, if possible, regardless of the product's price (received or anticipated). It is a matter of record and common experience that wages sometimes increase and decrease regardless of price levels. The explanation for this is neither the beneficence nor the perspicacity of the capitalist, since the latter is impossible and the former unprofitable in the short-run reality imposed by competition. The level of the wage typically increases when labor is scarce or powerful, and decreases when the class balance of power favors capital or when there is a greater number of people than jobs.

As a general rule, the wage varies with the organization and political power of labor. When unions and working class parties are weak, or workers for any reason are less militant in their demands, the wage can fail to the level of individual or family subsistence. When those organizations are strong and their members militant, the wage can rise until it intrudes unduly upon what capital takes as the portion of the surplus necessary to motivate it to reinvest rather than shift the portion it has already taken as its own profit to another enterprise or industry.

To be sure, labor creates the surplus by producing more than it needs to survive. But capital, by law and the history of its own struggle embodied in that law, owns it and can dispose of it virtually as it will. For the capitalist, the wage is a minimal payment intended to provide what the worker needs (or can demand) to continue working, no more. Anything greater than that amount is treated by capital as theft. When labor attempts to increase its portion of the surplus, either through contractual or extra-contractual means, capital will, among other tactics, intensify work by expanding workers' duties or speeding the work process, increase the length of the working day thereby increasing the number of hours of production the capitalist can claim over what must be allotted to the needs of workers, decrease the quality of labor's organization and depress the militancy of workers by means of legislation (the force of the state) or direct coercion, shift if possible to capital-intensive rather than labor-intensive production thereby reconstituting a needy labor force willing to accept any level of wage in order to survive, create an inflation that deprives the wage of its value relative to capital's gain through sales (an informal tax), institute a recession or depression creating competition among workers for scarce jobs, and/or force a shift in state expenditures from socially valid projects to support for the projects of capitalists.

It is clear that some of these measures are strictly economic and some political. The latter demonstrate the limits of labor struggles through collective bargaining over the size of the wage. It is also clear that the attempt to control labor inevitably enforces a recomposition of capital itself. For example, not every enterprise can be shifted to a capital-intensive basis; inflation may destroy the smaller segments of capital, as might recession or depression (cf. O'Connor 1973; Aglietta 1979; Kesselman 1982; Aronowitz 1983; Gordon et al. 1982a; Davis 1980a).

While it is true that "value" refers to society's capacity to produce for itself, and the value of a good depends upon the proportion of that capacity mobilized by a single producing unit, the discussion of money, commodities, and labor has not yet fully distinguished value from price. The reason is that those concepts were developed in regard to capital's reality. For the capitalist, the wage is a sum of money. It should now begin to be apparent that the wage is only represented by money; it is, relative to the needs of society, and hence the interest of labor, an expression of value.

This chapter has provided a preliminary analysis of the opposition of capital and human needs and a formulation in terms of the relationship between the production of commodities and the society of the producers. The following chapter shifts the analysis toward the concept of value so far as it relates to the sociological and social psychological significance of "labor power" and "exploitation." For now, it is clear that a feasible sociology must take as its immediate object of study what Marx called the "society of the producers," recognize in that "society" more than the assembly of those bearing labor power, though something less than an ensemble, and divide its study into two fundamental categories: 1. the character and likely ramifications of capital's inevitable attempt to contain the effects of its own contradictions, and 2. the forms of interaction and extended sociality that must characterize the "society of the producers." For the first, the empirical emphasis remains that of social control. For the second, research and analysis must proceed from the standpoint of collectivity mediated by capital-imposed cooperation, regardless of how particularized the units studied might be. It is this second category that is discussed in chapters 9 and 10 of this book.

Notes

1. "Both this transformation [of money to means of subsistence] and the subsequent consumption of these commodities as use-values constitute a process that has no *direct* bearing on the immediate process of production, or, more precisely, the labour process, and which in fact operates outside its limits" (Marx 1976, p. 983).

2. One of the ways it acknowledges that society is by liberal theories of "distribution." The fact that such theories make the category error of confusing a collection of people with their social formation makes the acknowledgment one of form but not content, and the acknowledged form part of the onesidedness of capital's perspective.

3. Volume 3 of *Capital* is Marx's fullest discussion of this series of "best cases." It is his exploration of the implications of the capitalist mode of production as a whole and should not be read as an attempt to describe an existing or empirically likely state of affairs, despite the temptation to do so as a result of its uncanny accuracy as a representation of "late capitalism."

4. "Ultimate," as used above, does not mean "in the last analysis," or "eventually," or "at the extreme." It means as a deep and ever-present aspect of the social, economic, and political reality of capitalism. Contradiction and conflict are ultimate in the sense of being ever-present, not in the sense of being eventual.

5. Marx's use of the expression "socially necessary labor time" refers not to the time needed to do something but to the portion of society's fund of time exacted by capital in order to produce one thing or another.

6

Value, Labor, Exploitation

GIVEN THAT THE exchange of goods and therefore the realization of their value depends upon social labor, it should be clear that capitalist wealth must consist of more than money if its accumulation is to make a difference to capital as such. Even the surplus value, what is uniquely produced by human labor beyond what is necessary to support it, is realized as value only to the extent to which it can be converted through sales into a further productive employment of labor. Since the productivity of labor is the result of its socialization as labor power, cooperation, and the society of production, the value of a good has something to do with its relative contribution to the social aspect of production. This is why the capitalist's economically obligatory indifference to the quality or type of good produced is a problem for the actual expansiveness of capital and the accumulation of significant, value-realizing wealth.

At the least, a product must provide a profit to its seller over the costs of its production, in particular the cost of the labor that went into it; and this must be realized as an investable surplus. But this requirement applies to the local problems of given enterprises. For capitalists to profit in general, and the wealth represented by profit to grow in its capacity to mobilize labor, the economy must produce the kinds of goods necessary for its own stability and steadiness of growth: capital goods, goods that satisfy the social needs of the "society of the producers," goods that satisfy the administrative needs of capitalist enterprise. But, as we have seen, production for sale and profit can only be indifferent to needs, even its own. The market militates against the general requirement because it is both an unsocialized collection of local transactions and a monetary standardization of what are otherwise significant qualitative differences among tasks and products. On the other hand, it is capital's only device for expanding production; without it the accumulation of wealth is impossible as a private accumulation of capital.

Yet production can proceed and advance only if the freedom of the market is qualified by some assessment of the suitability of productive activity to the needs of the total economy, and such an assessment can only come from a position external to the market and independent of the single enterprise. Any such qualification must be generalized, however, and therefore can only undermine the rationality of the local enterprises so far as their immediate situations are concerned. Capital has, of course, expanded—though only with a corresponding centralization and concentration—in every period of its development; and this expansion has always involved qualifications of the freedom of capitalists in general. It is an irony of "free enterprise" that various fractions of capital have been able to protect their market positions and maintain productivity only by sponsoring policies inconsistent with that freedom and thus with the "laws" of the free market. Trusts, protective tariffs, the protection of monopolies through license and subsidy, and the development of central statelike banks are among the devices that have restricted the "freedom" of enterprise in order to respond to crises in the relationship between the uses of money and the determination of what is and what is not to be produced.

The productive process of society is greater than any single enterprise and different from the sum of enterprises. Whether the sale of products can lead to further production depends upon what can be done with the money for which they are sold. To the extent to which that money is a valid index of the value of the good for which it is exchanged, to the extent to which it represents the collective work that actually goes into such production, it represents as well a general productive capacity. But that will depend upon its relation to the cost of labor used in the specific production of the good, the most general costs of production to the society as a whole, and the consistency and reliability of the market as a fund of connected goods. In regard to this last requirement, a product can only be purchased if the buyer has or can get other commodities whose use, or purchase regardless of use, is at least in principle related to it: one buys a car only if it is possible to buy gas, find parking space, have somewhere to go, and be reassured by the stability of the market itself that all these adjunct conditions will be sustained over time. Thus, the sale of any commodity depends upon the integrity of the market and therefore the reliability of the productive processes of society as a whole. It follows that the sale, in general, of goods for money may not realize their value—productive capacity employed or withdrawn from society—and therefore may not be a condition of further and/or expanded production. That credit, promises, and what Marx called "fictional" money (or capital) are instituted to guarantee the continuation of production only exacerbates the crises inherent in the mediation of the relations of production and exchange by the market (cf. Marx 1981b, part 5).

If the credit system appears as the principal lever of overproduction and excessive speculation in commerce, this is simply because the reproduction process, which is elastic by nature, is now forced to its most extreme limit; and this is because a great part of the social capital is applied by those who are not its owners, and who therefore proceed quite unlike owners who, when they function themselves, anxiously weigh the limits of their private capital. This only goes to show how the valorization of capital founded on the antithetical character of capitalist production permits actual free development only up to a certain point, which is constantly broken through by the credit system. The credit system hence accelerates the material development of the productive forces and the creation of the world market, which it is the historical task of the capitalist mode of production to bring to a certain level of development, as material foundations for the new form of production. At the same time, credit accelerates the violent outbreaks of this contradiction, crises, and with these the elements of dissolution of the old mode of production. [Marx 1981b, p. 572]

Similarly, the usefulness of money, the possibility of its being invested, is related to fluctuations in the general price level, the availability to the investor of labor, materials, and equipment, and opportunities for speculation. The first two depend upon production processes in society at large. The third has to do with the relative autonomy of the money tokens (bills, coins, and so on) from the actual value they represent: people often hoard money, collect it, speculate, or invest it in the production of goods, such as weapons, gadgets, and luxury items, that deplete rather than increase the overall productive capacity of society.

This is by no means an exhaustive discussion of the difference between price (represented by sums of money substitutes, or tokens) and value (the part of society's productive capacity that is used to produce a given type of commodity). It is only intended to indicate a problem: money may circulate independently of the value it represents, and because of this, discrepancies may arise between price and value that undermine the capacity of the market to provide incentives for productive investment. For example, any unplanned devaluation of a nation's coin makes it difficult for the prior sale of a good to realize a return to its productive capacity. Attempts to deal with this problem, intrinsic as it is to capitalism, can only exacerbate it—as the histories of speculation, depression, recession, inflation, monopoly, and unemployment show only too well.

The capitalist usually says that the value of a good is the cash that its sale can bring. But this is, as we have seen, too limited a concept of value to account for how the economy works as a whole. It corresponds only to the immediate practical situation of the individual capitalist, constrained by competition and the exigencies of debt. If we are to have an economic theory that has practical implications for society as a whole, the term "value" must be defined in relation to concepts adequate to the description of "society." Concepts adequate only to particular situations (and aggregates of situations) will not do.

We have seen that the capitalist has the advantage of what his or her workers have produced only if specific types of other goods are being produced and the market is fluid and reasonably intact. Goods have value, in the technical sense, only if their production supports and/or leads to an increase in the general level of production.The value of a particular good depends upon the value that is used in its production; it therefore reflects an investment not merely by the individual owner but by the total society of production on which he or she depends. Indeed, the general product of capitalist production is *value* in the sense of increased productive capacity. Therefore, value in this general sense depends upon the continual socialization of the productive process and therefore presumably upon the socialization of productive property. This is why policies intended to rationalize the market can only have short-term benefits at best and must eventually contribute to the crisis that they aim to mitigate, the societal realization of value in the face of the private disposition of products and money.

The fact that the capitalist economy can only work when it produces enough goods, and of the kinds that enhance its capacity further to produce, means that everything depends on the convertibility of money (already a conversion of value) to value, by the purchase of new facilities, the maintenance of old ones, and the reemployment of labor under conditions that are adequate to the general needs of the society of producers. But because each capitalist makes an individual decision in the light of immediate and local prospects of monetary gain, and in the light of opportunities both to reinvest in production and to speculate in a variety of productive and nonproductive enterprises, the prices of things will vary somewhat independently of their value and in ways that cannot be controlled without deliberately linking the use of money to the general conditions of production. When this uncontrolled variation of money occurs, and it always does to some degree or other, individualized profit-taking will be at least somewhat speculative and in any case inconsistent with the requirements of production in general.

Thus, private ownership of the means of production and private control of the surplus produced by labor (the resource that we have been calling "wealth") tend to undermine the social conditions of production and hence society. Capitalist enterprise is in this way inconsistent with its own context and the conditions of its existence. This is where the critique of capital has led us. It is the central and indisputable finding of Marxism and the reason why the Marxian intellectual tradition has been so influential. The discrepancy between price and value is one manifestation of that contradiction, itself an expression of the incompatibility of social production with the private control of what is produced.

CRISES AND SOCIALIST MOVEMENTS

This makes it possible to describe capitalist society in a way that corresponds to a dynamic conception of its historicity: as a volatile movement of social forces through successions of increasingly inclusive and extreme crises. In virtually every case, the result is a retrenchment of capital by eliminating productive facilities, undermining labor's political power, and "disciplining" the labor force through unemployment and lowered wages. In virtually every case, there is a consolidation of the most powerful sectors of capital, the destruction of its own competitive base (small business), and the introduction of coercive measures to ensure adequate protection against society for the new concentrations of wealth.

The periodicity of these crises represents, for surviving capitalists, the "business cycle." For workers it represents the unreliability of the wage economy and a corresponding insecurity of life's conditions. For society, it represents both danger and opportunity—the danger of coercive and totalizing attempts by those in power to manage chaos in their own interest, and the opportunity, democratic or not, for reorganization and reformation. This century has seen the danger— fascism, the "new right," the destruction of the economic viability of the Third World through fiscal policies aimed at protecting the vested interests of capital, and a United States foreign policy consistently reactionary and hostile to social planning in favor of the further domination of poor nations by immense first-world banks and corporations. It has also seen the opportunity and problems implicit in socialist planning, given Andrew Levine's "minimalist" definition of "socialism":

> Socialism is defined here in relation to capitalism. It supposes capitalism's already substantial victory over political economic arrangements based on the division of society into economically significant estates. Capitalism requires formal equality of persons—to the extent that persons must be able to become wage laborers and, more generally, to enter into contractual relations. Socialism takes over the formal equality capitalism has secured, while radically altering capitalism's other distinctive feature: the private ownership of society's principal means of production. Socialism is post-capitalism; capitalism without private property in means of production. The abolition of private property in means of production is part of what all, or very nearly all, socialists intend in speaking of socialism. . . .

However, it is well to distinguish values socialists hope to realize under socialism—values generally shared with pro-capitalists—from socialism itself" (Levine 1984, pp. 6-7).

The danger from the right has always been clear. It has included the degradation of popular democratic institutions in favor of unregulated "private enterprise," militarism in the conduct of the foreign and domestic affairs of state, the transformation of governments into instruments of domination, and the subjection of national populations to debt costs and fiscal obligations that neither derive from their needs nor are consistent with the needs and prospects of their societies. Attempts to implement socialism have varied considerably according to circumstance, the character of the social movements from which they have stemmed, aspects of the histories upon which socialists have built, and upon other conditions too numerous to list. They have nevertheless provided instances of improved social stability, increased development of the social forces of production, improvements in the quality of life, and greater participation in government. It goes without saying that these attempts have been uneven as well as varied, reflecting external and historical conditions rather than an abstract "nature of the socialist enterprise" (cf. Moffit 1983; Amin 1982; Aglietta 1979; Block 1977; Payer 1982; Mandel 1980; Cohen and Rogers 1983; Levine 1984; Petras 1985; and cf. discussions regularly appearing in *New Left Review, Socialism and Democracy, Telos, Kapitalistate, Monthly Review,* and *Socialism in the World*).

While it is still too early to judge most of these experiments, a great deal has been written about the problems that must be solved if socialism is to succeed to any degree, and about the ways in which those problems have been addressed in the major "social democratic" and postrevolutionary societies. One of the practical implications of Marxian theory is that regardless of the problems of realizing a nonexploitive, cooperative, economy in the present global situation, the experiments are virtually inevitable and in any case necessary because the danger is otherwise extreme and perhaps unavoidable. The hostility of capital to society is itself inevitable within the contradictory mode of production—the exploitive class relation—that is capital's base.

If Marx and the Marxian tradition are correct in their analysis of the capitalist mode of production, socialist movements must address three decisive problems in terms of the character and development of class-based conflicts within the contemporary global situation: 1. the burdens faced by populations due to an increasingly global capitalist accumulation (cf. Wallerstein 1974; Frank 1969; Amin 1976); 2. the lack of clear models for a strategy of successive policies that can accumulate as conditions of a socialist rather than some other type of transformation (cf. Poulantzas 1978; Mandel 1980; Petras 1985); 3. the need for institutional bases for the societally valid politics appropriate to such a strategy (cf. Cohen and Rogers 1983; Piven and Cloward 1977; Laclau and Mouffe 1985; Aronowitz 1981; Hall 1977; Wolfe 1977, 1981; Gordon et al. 1982). This means on the one hand building the political instruments necessary for the struggle (including associations, organizations, and coalitions that may or may not reflect the older imperatives of nation, party, or union), and on the other, supporting policies that increase the degree and societally progressive quality of social control over the means and results of production. It also means, from an ideological point of view, taking a stance toward revolutionary activities in the world directed against capitalist expansion that judges them historically rather than by absolutist standards (cf. Levine 1984; Hobsbawm 1973; Blackburn 1978).

While this is a minimal program if society is to overcome the conditions that undermine its viability, the historical limitations of even its most radical version require that all socialist movements operate in regard to those limitations. Labor, as a class and as a base for socialist politics, is "labor" as constituted within capitalism; the productive order that makes socialism possible is one that reflects the creation of society both by capital and through the history of class struggle. It is, therefore, an order of large-scale, integrated production; the political mechanism for transforming that productive order to the socialized order already implicit in it is somehow connected with what we recognize as "the state," with all the problems that entails and all the limitations it imposes upon the process of bringing the relations of production (ownership and control) into line with the forces of production (labor and its social organization).

What is clear is that the transition to some form of socialism is both necessary and difficult: the divisions of the world, the persistent hegemony of capital, and the destructiveness of the various wars—Vietnam, the war against Central America—by which representatives of capital have attempted to make manifest that hegemony ensure that the transition will be conflictful and often dispiriting and that there will be periods when reaction will threaten the gains of the past. Marxian theory contributes a sense of the historical limits of this struggle by analyzing the aspect of capital that is implicit in the socialization of labor and therefore in the labor of creating socialism. Beyond that aspect, at the edge of practice, Marxian theory reinforces the attitudes of self-criticism and respect for the historicity of all acts that are essential to a theoretically uncertain but practically unavoidable politics.

TOWARD A PHENOMENOLOGY OF LABOR POWER

We have yet to consider the implications of capitalist wealth for a sociologically significant identification of "labor," though we have discussed the socialization of labor as a productive force and a class relation. To the capitalist, labor is a cost of production no different from any other cost and measured as an outlay of money: the motivation of the worker, the type of work being performed, its quality, and its tradition as craft or occupation have no significance beyond their bearing on cost. The individuality of the worker and the concrete activity actually involved in production are as irrelevant to the capitalist as the tangible difference between coins and bills. They are only incidentally and arbitrarily related to what the capitalist hopes to gain if he or she is to remain a capitalist.

Marx pointed out that the identification of "labor" as a monetary cost arises from the inevitably short-sighted and necessarily localized perspective of capital in the production of commodities. It shifts the capitalist's interest from the qualitatively *concrete* work that individual workers do to something about work that is entirely *abstract* and capable of measurement and quantitative rationalization. The implementation of any task involves the coordination of various skills, activities, and judgments. But taken as one of the capitalist's costs of production this resolves itself economically to an outlay of money in terms of which different costs are combined and used to evaluate the profitability of an investment. When this is considered in general,

> the labour objectified in the values of commodities is not just presented negatively, as labour in which abstraction is made from all the concrete forms and useful properties of actual work. Its own positive nature is explicitly brought out, namely the fact that it is the reduction of all kinds of actual labour to their common character of being human labour in general, of being the expenditure of human labour-power (Marx 1976, pp. 159–60).

Concrete labor consists of the specific activities involved in making something distinct. These can only be described qualitatively and in relation to the useful qualities of the product. The same activities subsumed under the category of cost can only be described quantitatively, without regard to their necessarily distinctive characteristics, or their relation to the special qualities of their product. As such, they are abstracted in the sense of being taken as applications of a general and undifferentiated capacity to produce anything.

Economics that recognizes concrete labor emphasizes what people do and why they do it; economics that recognizes only the abstraction of labor emphasizes results, and only those results that can be summarized as a desocialized relation of costs to income. Only the former can be said to be a human or social science. The latter is a "science" of things, the accountant's science. Put in different terms, for the first, people are ends rather than means; for the second they are only means to ends that they can neither have nor share.

In any case, because it is the capitalist's interest to produce goods for profitable sale (and therefore to transform qualitatively distinct concrete work into abstract labor), it is that interest, so far as its practice is historically feasible, that organizes and controls modern production as such: capitalist production depends upon the type of labor appropriate to production exclusively for monetary profit, namely abstract labor or labor as a cost of capitalist production. But then, "The capitalist cost of the commodity is measured by the expenditure of *capital,* whereas the actual cost of the commodity is measured by the expenditure of *labour*" (Marx 1981, p. 118). This is a juridical as well as an economic and social fact, and it is impossible to separate the economy of abstract labor from the class strategies by which it is enforced and the ideological perspectives that support that enforcement:

> The use of a commodity belongs to its purchaser, and the seller of labour-power, by giving his labour, does no more, in reality, than part with the use-value he has sold. From the instant he steps into the workshop, the use-value of this labour-power and therefore also its use, which is labour, belongs to the capitalist. By the purchase of labour-power, the capitalist incorporates labour, as a living agent of fermentation, into the lifeless constituents of the product, which also belong to him. From his point of view, the labour process is nothing more than the consumption of the commodity purchased, i.e. of labour-power; but he can consume this labour-power only by adding the means of production to it. The labour-process is a process between things the capitalist has purchased, things which belong to him. Thus the product of this process belongs to him just as much as the wine which is the product of the process of fermentation going on in his cellar. [Marx 1976, p. 292]

This is not a general characterization of labor or a necessary condition of production per se, but labor's objective situation in relation to capital. It is what labor must be in the social relations of capitalist production. It is, as well, a given for the individual laborers who know themselves primarily through the conditions of their employment by another who represents a hostile interest (manifested by the market in labor power). The indifference of the capitalist toward the individual laborer and his or her particular work (concrete labor) is a necessary indifference, itself derived from the social relations of a commodity-producing economy. It is not a trait of individual capitalists but a trait capitalists must display in their economic actions if they are effectively to compete and effectively to appropriate and use the surplus created by socialized labor. What concerns the capitalist as capitalist is not what workers do but what they can be made to do under the constantly changing conditions of profitable enterprise.

This calls attention to the most general social psychological attribute of workers under capitalism: they must work toward an end they have not chosen, and one whose achievement will be neither to their credit nor to their benefit, indeed, ultimately to their detriment. For example, workers in a plant produce goods that are then sold by the owner for a profit. At a certain level of accumulation the capitalist must consider shifting investment from that productive center to more profitable opportunities that may have become available for the accumulated surplus, regardless of the consequent unemployment of the workers who provided the profit in the first place. The more productive the workers, the faster the accumulation (other things remaining equal), the more likely the shift, and the greater the insecurity and loss they ultimately experience. In this sense, workers under capitalism work not only for the capitalist but against themselves.

This is not an inevitable predicament or a reflection of human nature: it is not a condition of modernization as such, nor does it represent "the necessary pangs of progress." It is the result of an economy in which the majority of people own nothing but their capacity to expend energy and must sell that capacity as a commodity in order to live. But then it is a feature of an historically unique mode of production.

The need and ability to sell one's energy (one's capacity to work regardless of the specific task and product) and thereby yield to any purpose the buyer imposes is capital's most generally useful resource, the essential ingredient of both commodity production and that mobilization of "the society of the producers" that allows the production of commodities to supervene all socio-political boundaries. What capital employs is then not a number of individual laborers but a portion of the total social pool of undifferentiated labor power, a source of energy that is free of normal, self-reflecting, societal limitations on human conduct—motivational, emotional, aesthetic, interpersonal, and moral—and measured, imperfectly as a cost to society and as a rough approximation of the depletion of the pool by any given instance of employment, in units of time.

Labor power is the commodity form of abstracted labor. It is that product of past labor (the labor involved in sustaining the laborer and his or her society) that the laborer has to sell. The wage is not intended to support the individual worker as a person but to sustain his or her capacity to expend effort in the production of more than he or she needs. Nor is the wage a cost intended to sustain concrete exercises of skill and commitment, but the capacity to continue to expend effort on whatever purpose capital accumulation imposes. The fact that all work resolves itself to labor power is the distinctive property of human productive activity under capitalism. It is capital's most original historical creation and its continuing practical foundation.

"The worker" is someone who sells his or her portion of a socially constituted energy (labor power) for a purpose to be determined by the capitalist according to conditions of accumulation as they appear in the local situation of production and competition. A capitalist who employs workers for a particular enterprise must nevertheless be understood socioeconomically as dipping into a labor pool, an undifferentiated mass of labor power, for energy to be deployed in privately controlled operations that contribute solely to the expansion of the employer's capital through an expropriation of surplus value. Capitalist production proceeds, then, through the harnessing of surplus-producing human energy (labor power) to tools (means of production) owned by the capitalist.

Since the means of production no less than labor power itself are products of past human labor, there is no point at which the capitalist and his or her wealth are not dependent upon and beholden to labor. What nevertheless guarantees the capitalist's control over the production process and its product is its legally sanctioned, economically substantiated, and technologically implemented control over the individuals who have had to sell their portion of energy (labor power) in order to survive. Workers who resist that control can, in principle, be replaced by more compliant workers drawn from the labor pool. In this way, capital's social and political discipline over the work force, and therefore its control over the population of its society, is built into the economics of production.

Because labor under capitalism is the quantity labor power, because it is nevertheless socialized as a society of producers, because both are aspects of unavoidable social relations of production, and because the instrumentalities for sustaining those relations require economic and political policies that are directed at these conditions, the critique of capital is not just economics but sociology and politics. Because the analysis of capital yields social relations that are historically specific and are at the same time conditions of knowing and analyzing capitalism, the condition of labor is the unique perspective that allows theory both to encompass the ensemble of relations that comprise capitalism as its condition of historical transformation and to be verified as self-critique through practice.

At the same time, because labor power is itself a commodity that must be sold if its value is to be realized, it is legitimate to consider the situation of its seller and necessary to consider that situation from the

point of view of the paradoxical dissolution of individuality and concrete activity in the capitalist transformation of labor to labor power.

THE REPLACEABILITY OF THE LABORER:
A SOCIAL PSYCHOLOGY OF LABOR

This arrangement subjects the laborer's energy to exploitation and
makes the individual laborer expendable. Individual workers have
recognizable status within the capitalist economy only as the bearers of
energy, labor power. Ordinary people, "the common people," "the
workers," have become prominent in social science only to the extent
to which their political actions, not their skills or interests, have forced
capital to make distinctions among them (as unionized or not, old or
young, domestic or foreign, and so on). Given that status, workers are
replaceable as individuals: all they have to offer are units of energy that
are the same in principle as all other such units. To the extent to which
the human component of labor power, its embodiment in an individual
human being with loyalties, interests, affections, needs, and the rest,
qualifies the mobility of the energy or power component, it must be
depressed, suppressed, or replaced. Indeed, those consequences are
unavoidable if capital is to expand and capitalists are to accumulate
wealth. This interest in the control of the human component requires
technology that makes individual skills increasingly irrelevant to the
actual process of production, and an organization of work such that the
individual worker is increasingly deprived of the opportunity to make
precisely those decisions that most affect his or her life (cf. Gutman
1976; Clawson 1980; Braverman 1975; Aronowitz 1973; Montgomery
1979; Burowoy 1979; Edwards 1979; Seashore 1954; Marx 1976,
chaps. 14 and 15).

> John Stuart Mill says in his *Principles of Political Economy:* "It is
> questionable if all the mechanical inventions yet made have lightened the
> day's toil of any human being." That is, however, by no means the aim of
> the application of machinery under capitalism. Like every other instru-
> ment for increasing the productivity of labour, machinery is intended to
> cheapen commodities and, by shortening the part of the working day in
> which the worker works for himself, to lengthen the other part, the part he
> gives to the capitalist for nothing. The machine is a means for producing
> surplus value. [Marx 1976, p. 492]

On a different, extra-local, scale of social relations, it is why the
agencies of capital, such as they are, tend to promote a societal
rationalization that emphasizes mass rather than collectivity (through
education, the media, and politics) and is therefore inimical to the sort
of self-conscious participation in the political economy in which even

routine and detail jobs can be experienced as principled action relevant to the development of the society of producers (cf. Blum and McHugh 1984; Braverman 1975). Thus, the technical and social sterilization of the capitalist labor process is part of the more general disposition of capital to separate work from other aspects of society and contributes to the socially generalized alienation of labor (cf. Willis 1977).[1] It is part of the generalization of exploitation as a social relation through an historic process (a class "project") that divides work and leisure, workplace and home, men and women, family and individual, production and consumption, activity and participation, and economy and society, and operates against the prospect of societal redemption that is nevertheless invoked by this process as a feature of the dialectic of exploitation. Despite its importance in reinforcing the socialization of work and workers, thereby contributing to the political aspect of the class relation, the working day has become one of the major health problems of the epoch, inimical to what psychologists identify as basic conditions of emotional health, identity, self-conscious learning, and personality growth (cf. Braverman 1975; Gordon et al. 1982). Its organization places difficult if not impossible burdens on marriage and family, new strains on extra-familial relationships among competing workers, and new limitations on political participation and everyday life (cf. Aronowitz 1973; Edwards 1979; Braverman 1975; Brown 1978; Rubin 1978). Even the socially integrative aspects of the workplace, whatever their positive effects, yield only guarded affections (cf. Willis 1977).

ALIENATION AND BODILY POSSESSION

These are results of a production process that can be expressed in other ways as well. The point is that the process must have some such social psychological result if it is to depend upon the exploitation of labor as labor power and as the society of producers. There is, in other words, a subjective side to the objective replaceability of the worker. Two aspects are of particular social psychological significance: 1. First is the pervasive sense of insecurity that workers experience, a sense of having no indelible rights, of being one of many and an instance of a type, of lacking control over one's fate, of being subordinate to machines and therefore less important than things: "In fact the rule of the capitalist over the worker is nothing but the rule of the independent *conditions of labour* over the *worker,* conditions that have made themselves independent of him" (Marx 1976 p. 989). 2. Second is the realization, normally below the level of verbalization, of an absolute separation of productive purpose (the direction and ordering of conduct) from productive behavior (the concrete use of energy). The individual's personal experience reflects the fact that his or her daily life is under the control of other indistinct but overwhelming powers, and serves purposes that are foreign to it.

> In terms of effort, of the expenditure of his life's energy, work is the personal activity of the worker. But as something which *creates value,* as something involved in the process of objectifying labour, the worker's labour becomes one of the *modes of existence* of capital, it is incorporated into capital as soon as it enters the production process. . . . Consequently it spells the impoverishment of the worker who creates value as *value alien to himself.* [Ibid., p. 988]

Indeed, "Work can only be wage-labour when its *own* material conditions confront it as autonomous powers, alien property . . ." (ibid., p. 1006).

We can examine some of the implications of this alienation through the metaphor of demonic possession. The body, during the periods of its sale and utilization, that is, during the working day, becomes in effect a thing. Its activities are motions disconnected from the self and from that self's deliberations. One who lives by selling his or her labor power and then enacting another's purpose is subjectively dispossessed as a self and replaced by an entirely foreign agency:

> This purchase and sale of labour power implies that the objective conditions of labour—i.e. the *means of subsistence* and the *means of production*—are separated from the living labour-power itself. . . . This separation is so radical that these conditions . . . appear as *independent persons* confronting the worker. [Ibid., p. 1017]

Demonic possession is an apt metaphor for this sort of alienation. "Possession," in its occult sense, typically meant that a person's body is taken over by an intention so foreign to the intentions of the dispossessed self that the body's behavior is irrelevant or hostile to its own dispositions, as in a fit. "By incorporating living labour-power into the material constituents of capital, the latter becomes an animated monster and it starts to act 'as if consumed by love' " (ibid., p. 1007). Similarly, the possessed victim's acts were said to manifest the overwhelming will of another and compelling purposes yet at odds with those he or she would otherwise choose.

The reference to the demonic is not essential to the experience of this self-alienation. Plausible representation of the separation of purpose and activity, the subjective aspect of an objective fact, varies with culture and history. It is the separation that is important, and the consequent loss of embodiment; and the modern redemption of the victim proceeds, not by occult means such as exorcism, but more generally as a reconstitution or normalization of the person as a recognizable whole through the elimination, disguise, displacement, or distortion of whatever evidences the power of foreign agency (cf. Goffman 1963, for a discussion of the varieties of redemption).

The culture of capitalism is replete with examples of these forms of redemption, adequate testimony to the separation itself. Hyperactive leisure as surrogate concrete work activity, images of the heroic that disguise domination, self-deceiving forms of assertiveness such as scapegoating and patriotism, and the easy acceptance of new forms of domination for old are cases in point. Denigrating those who refuse to submit to hostile purposes is, probably, the most consistent self-denying elision of one's own subordination: witness the undifferentiating anticommunism and hostility toward domestic protest and Third World revolutions expressed by many who nevertheless share the victimization against which protesters and revolutionaries have tried to organize opposition.

Regardless of the forms redemption takes, what is important is the fact that there is an objective basis for a common sense of being inhabited, being out of one's own control, lacking coherent identity, being unable to experience the growth of the self, being subject always to the will of another. This might explain a common feature of "authoritarianism" in which the victim, in turn, subjects others to domination. It might also help to explain the ideological importance of the myth of the hero-champion in the contemporary American mythos well-documented in sports pages, films, political speeches, and popular novels. The champion is what one "would be" or "could be" but is not: exempt from domination and free of historical constraint.

On the other hand, the alienation of purpose has something to do with the persistence of protest in the capitalist context: exploitation and domination are not always so easily disguised or distorted. Still, it is perhaps not untoward to suggest that one characteristic ailment of people in capitalism is not so much being "out of one's mind," as being *in* the mind of another: in this case, one might identify a "manic" pole in hyperactive avoidance and a "depressive" pole in hyperpassive acquiescence. Regardless of the extremes, something of this sort must be subjectively valid for those who "bear" their labor power to the market and submit to the body's capture by those who purchase and therefore own that power.

The alienation of labor, the separation of the worker from his or her activity and its products, is the experience of those who must sell their labor power in order to survive, the majority of people living under capitalism. The subjective aspect must be something akin to possession, but today, with the force of economic necessity that marks the worker with a replaceability even more certain and irresistible than the irrelevance of soul that marks the victims of demons:

> The means of production made use of by the worker in the actual labour process are, it is true, the property of the capitalist, and they therefore confront his labour, which is the only expression of his life, as *capital* . . . On the other hand, however, it is he who makes use of them in the course of his work. In the actual process, the worker uses the means of labour as his tools, and he uses up the object of labour in the sense that it is the material in which his labour manifests itself. . . . The situation looks quite different in the valorization process. Here it is not the worker who makes use of the means of production, but the means of production that make use of the worker. . . . The means of production thus become no more than leeches drawing off as large an amount of living labour as they can. [Marx 1976, p. 988]

To be the body of another's purpose is to be a means, a tool, a thing, and thus to know one's self as replaceable by other things. To know that purposive Other as something beyond what is usually meant by personality and as implacable as economic necessity is to know one's self amidst the experience of that self's futility; and with that knowledge comes a self-denying gratitude for the small mercies of life occasionally found by those who have no rights and can offer nothing concrete in exchange. It is no wonder that capitalism has generated its own forms of enchantment in new religions and curiously antisocial and antihumanist versions of past ones.

> Thus at the level of material production, of the life-process in the realm of the social—for that is what the process of production is—we find the *same* situation that we find in *religion* at the ideological level, namely the inversion of subject into object and *vice versa*. Viewed *historically* this inversion is the indispensable transition without which wealth as such, i.e. the relentless productive forces of social labour, which alone can form the material base of a free human society, could not possibly be created by force at the expense of the majority. This antagonistic stage cannot be avoided, any more than it is possible for man to avoid the stage in which his spiritual energies are given a religious definition as powers independent of himself. What we are confronted by here is the *alienation* . . . of man from his own labour. [Ibid., p. 990]

The replaceability of individuals is a derivative of exploitation where the total economy is organized in regard to the production of goods for the private accumulation of wealth, where exploitation is an unavoidable condition of life (Ollman 1971; Jacoby 1975; Schneider 1975).

Summary

The sense of being replaceable is the result of a general condition that is experienced locally, by individuals or groups in particular situations that pertain to capitalist production. It involves a translation or transformation of the general requirements of capitalist economy into obligations, practices, and forms of representation that influence people in their jobs, in their families, on special occasions, and in the ordinary conversational activities by means of which they validate their mutality (cf. Goffman 1961a; Willis 1977; cf. below, chapters 9 and 10).

The key to understanding the experience of replaceability in non-work environments has to do with those aspects of culture and language that are laden with the logic of exchange: the putative privacy of purpose that is analogous to the privacy of property, the incessant comparisons by individuals of one another according to general standards of "performance," and other strictly organizational/managerial matters that presume the possible exchangeability of individuals as things, and the use of type-names or credentials indelibly to mark persons, places, things, and events, as cases, instances of genre, or legitimate encumbents to a claim of official license. These are not merely reflections of the complexity of modern social life. They are comprehensible in their generality only within the capitalist version of society, only on condition that "exploitation" is the fundamental link of "person" to "society."

This discussion illustrates possible ramifications of exploitation (taken, for the moment, in abstraction from the dialectic of capitalist production) beyond the context of waged work itself. On the other hand, it is precisely that context that establishes its more general significance.[2]

It is important to note that the experiences associated with exploitation vary within fairly narrow limits, according to circumstance, setting, and personal and local history. One does not understand the theory of exploitation better by discussing those experiences; but some recognition of them is necessary in order to appreciate the phenomenology and sociology of exploitation. The sense of being objectified in exploitation may appear below the level of verbalization in gestures, the covert selection of safe conversational strategies in regard to specific topics and settings, and the clandestine ordering of priorities within groups and in the more inchoate reaches of daily life. It may yield feelings of betrayal, theft, victimization, injustice, or a desire for the relief of childhood, play, leisure or unambiguous authority. It is as likely to lead to scapegoating and resentment as to rebellion and socialist politics.

We have already seen that "exploitation" refers to the objective relations of labor and capital. Those who labor produce more than is needed for their support as individuals; but they labor only in cooperation with their fellows on the scale of the society of production. Self-realization is, then, possible only on condition that society itself is realized, something impossible when its capabilities are controlled by private parties for their own interests and that control is reinforced by law (cf. Miliband 1969; Hay 1975).

The immediate impact of exploitation on those who must sell their labor power in order to live, a sense of replaceability, insecurity, and being subject to a fate beyond one's control or the control of one's own society, is only one aspect of its sociology. Another, as we have seen, is the poverty that stems from the contradiction between the need for a *social* "distribution" of the surplus and the private and therefore *socially* unresponsive character of the control of that "distribution." The condition of the working class in general declines as capitalism matures. But what Marx and Engels called the "immiseration" of that class is not to be understood simply as the impoverishment of individuals, though it includes that, at least on a global scale. It is the increasing control of societal wealth and the domination of social life by private parties (individuals, corporations and so on) who have no obligation to support the society that supports them. What capital makes truly miserable is the most exploited portion of its working class; what is impoverishes is the cooperative aspect and collective prospects of its whole society.

Notes

1. Criticisms of "labor process theory," the analysis of the labor process in terms of the controls it imposes on workers and its constant conversion of work into labor power, have pointed to several problems. Among them are 1. the failure to examine the subjective dimension of the labor process, 2. the failure, therefore, to provide indices of resistence, 3. the failure to account for new technology and its recollectivization of the work group, 4. the overemphasis on factory and factorylike labor, and 5. an overly mechanistic view of the ways in which class relations are "reproduced." Whatever the value of these criticisms, it remains clear that the analysis of labor process as controls initiated by Braverman's classic study (1975), provides an adequate illustration of the tendencies inherent in the capitalist organization of production. The important aspects of this analysis are the concepts that must be employed in the analysis of the new technologies and the various forms of resistance. It is, of course, crucial to avoid making the error of using an example of conceptualization (labor power, expansion of

capital, etc.)—of factory or white collar work—as a basis for an induction to a general tendency or law. Because factory work has become more routinized and deskilled does not mean that that particular way of cheapening labor and/or expanding capital will necessarily generalize. Similarly, because there has been an upgrading of the labor process in one industry or nation does not mean that the general level of work-related skill has not gone down. Finally, no one has found adequate measures of skill and decision in the fields of the new technologies. It is nevertheless possible to observe the sequence of new skills followed by its degradation in virtually every area in which the new technologies have been introduced.

2. An adequate account of these ramifications would not, of course, treat them as independent consequences but as tendencies subject to the mediation of other forces. A fuller sociology of exploitation would deal with both the tendencies of capitalist production and the historically constituted conditions of the realization of these tendencies in one form or another. Nevertheless, that sociology would have to begin as an exploration of the logic of capitalist expansion, as has been done so far.

7

Social Differentiation and Unity

THE DISCUSSION OF labor's capitalism bears on several aspects of capitalist society that are otherwise difficult to understand: notably (1) the persistence of intraclass social differences (cf. Wright 1978; Gordon et al. 1982a; Aronowitz 1983), and (2) the increasingly problematic character of civil arrangements—family, community, culture—previously thought to be relatively stable sources of social solidarity and commitment (cf. Poster 1978; Rubin 1978; Flacks and Turkel 1978; Brown 1978).

Social differentiation may result from various conditions, but its most general forms and significance under capitalism are connected with the mobilization and deployment of labor for the production of commodities. The economically positive effect of capitalism on culture has been the creation of a market-subjectivity, relatively easily mobilized and disarmed, represented as "mass culture," "public opinion," and "the public sphere." Because of the distortions of consciousness that accompany the capitalist organization of society, the societally negative cultural effects are more evident and more revealing of the contradictory aspects of the capitalist mode of production. These effects have included the use and then destruction of settlements and traditions, the concentration and then displacement of populations and facilities necessary for the generational continuity of domestic arrangements that are nevertheless officially endorsed—families, neighborhoods, communities, and the disturbance of interactional conditions necessary for primary social groupings of all sorts (but cf. Brown 1978). The disturbance of putatively settled culture, tradition, and homeliness has been a result not of "the left" and its "reactions to progress" but of the economically driving impulses of capital itself (cf. Marx and Engels 1948; Rude, 1964; Hammond and Hammond 1910; Marcuse 1964; Thompson 1963; Habermas 1975).[1]

When all other relations of production are excluded, exploitation determines the general composition, integration, and cultural prospects of the workforce. The societally positive aspect of this has to do with the development of the society of producers as the only possible societally self-determining agency of capitalism, and explains in part the shift in twentieth-century democratic theory and practice from individualist to collectivist conceptions of rights, obligations, and forms of participation in the governance of society. In this regard, the internal struggle to overcome divisions among workers is as much a part of the conflict of classes as the external encounter of class organizations. Abstractly, both can be said to socialize labor politically, as production socializes it economically.

The negative aspects of the relationship between exploitation and social differentiation are of more immediate concern. Gender and age categories are by no means unique to capitalism. But the forms they take *as significant features of capitalist economy* involve invidious distinctions based in part on "productivity" (Ecker, 1983). Because "productivity" is defined in capitalist economy as a benefit at the expense of society, as a contribution to desocialized wealth, as an increment to profit rather than a satisfaction of need, its use is strictly ideological. That is, the term is used abstractly to justify preexisting and overdetermined social distinctions as rational to the needs of human economy as such, as if the rationality of private accumulation can be generalized to cover the requirements of all possible socioeconomic arrangements. Since capitalist economy creates a kind of wealth that cannot provide for society as such, the use of "productivity" to determine standards for deploying labor is inevitably inappropriate to the fulfillment of the conditions of any authentic society. The coupling of those standards to existing social divisions can only reinforce them, or displace them in exaggerated form, by situating them within the domain of economic necessity. This in turn moves social differentiation from the settings of attitude and culture, where intergroup contact might be expected to reduce the invidiousness of its effects, to the more volatile settings of conflict over scarce resources—including employment opportunities, services, and so on—where it can only end by reinforcing itself (cf. Moffit 1983; Payer 1982).

Gender and age distinctions are convenient but by no means necessary devices for maintaining divisions among workers. While they provide ready-made conditions of wage and occupational discrimination, and therefore contribute to lowering the overall level of the wage by pitting workers against each other, they are, relative to the needs of capital, arbitrary and, at least in principle, dispensable. Thus, the effects of gender and age distinctions are occasionally challenged through reforms that reproduce worker competition at other locations and in regard to other criteria. For example, the current use of arbitrary credentialling (college degrees, test scores, and so on) for job placement is a displacement of the competitive division of workers from more conventional criteria.

Similarly, the mobility of capital—the fact that private, asocial ownership allows equipment, plant, and materials to be moved with only minimal regard to the effects on communities—undermines local order and culture and disturbs the development of the affections, solidarity, and shared projects necessary for reliability in everyday life and the development of political mobilizations. This is of course merely a contemporary manifestation of the epochal process of "freeing" labor by destroying all but the most narrow connections among people and between people and tasks. It is part of the history of labor's transformation to labor power and the laborers' transformation to competing bearers of the only commodity they can exchange for their survival.

Indeed, anything that contributes to dislocations and competition among workers—hunger, scarcity of jobs, social fragmentation, weak unions, constant reorganizations of technology—allows capital to increase its exploitation of society. While this is often planned, it is as often determined by the normal operations of the capitalist economy, in particular the flow of investment toward cheaper costs of production and the production of more exchangeable goods (cf. Braverman 1975; Gordon, et al. 1982a). Invidious distinction—racism, sexism, and discrimination by age—is difficult to cure under the best of circumstances. Under capitalism, it is virtually impossible since the divisions reflect, at least in part, the necessarily unceasing insecurity of mutually competitive workers in an inherently inequitable and unstable economy.

Patterns of discrimination may be reinforced by competition for jobs regardless of whether or not that competition is planned and regardless of whether or not there is a supporting ideology. At the same time they may, in turn, reinforce exploitation. For example, racism allows for a relatively clear indexing of workers that contributes to the maintenance of a "reserve army of labor," an unemployed and/or transient portion of the labor force that is normally available for employment at capital's discretion and for low pay. The relative poverty and insecurity of that reserve army—traditionally composed of not only poor white males, but also women, children, so-called minorities, and black people across an even greater span of age than other groups, as well as workers in much of what is called the Third World—allows capital to reduce the wage periodically by threatening to replace employed workers with workers who have been unemployed or underemployed (cf. Gordon et al. 1982a).

The same dynamic accounts, in large part, for the fragility of what otherwise appear to be established and valuable social arrangements. Because of its special vulnerability to economic change, the family is a paradigmatic example. First, family members are increasingly drawn into economic activities inconsistent with the traditions, joint projects, interpersonal discipline, solidarity, and affection upon which the development of family life presumeably depends. While the "Western" family is in many ways an oppressive form, it nevertheless provides in its peculiar isolating tendencies and intensity temporary and occasional relief from interpersonal distortions of the capitalist organization of society (cf. Poster 1974; Deleuze and Guattari 1977; Zaretsky 1976; Lasch 1977; but cf. Rubin 1978). From the standpoint of economy, family life has a great deal to do with distributing capital's cost of reproducing its labor force. It can do this, however, only to the extent that it leaves the family's intensive character intact, something difficult if not impossible in the face of divisive economic demands on family members as individuals.

Second, stability and order within the family depend upon the validity of the family budget and the corresponding reliability of individual behavior within the family's fiscal constitution. The validity of a family's budget depends upon its capacity to reconcile individual with group needs; and this varies with the size and predictability of the family income. Family conflict is often a result of the declining predictability of income independent of its absolute amount. While this usually reflects the declining value of money relative to the size of the wage, it also reflects the social obligations placed by capitalist institutions on individuals and the standards of living that have been politically achieved.

Even with a supportive economy, family members often are divided by different institutionally reinforced market obligations. Television has made it possible to stimulate demands on the family budget that cannot be easily absorbed. For example, it provides "culturelike" representations of age grades, style, and gender norms, and thereby creates a mixed market within the family that corresponds more to external forces than to the integrative needs of the family as a whole relative to the family budget. Purchasing activities are made elaborate and given the gloss of value through attempts by mass media to institute social norms—imposed rather than spontaneous to the group, designed rather than emergent and historical, managed rather than even partially democratic. When successful, as they often are, these establish a media-dependent culture of fashion and fetish that both heightens and de-socializes pleasure. The result is that family members acquire virtually unavoidable sociocultural obligations at the level of the mass population that make it difficult for them to compromise in the distribution and use of the family income without undermining their sense of affiliation beyond the family.

Third, that some family members work in and some work outside the home creates different interests in domestic order and different senses of the proper ecology and practice of the household. This division arose historically as people were forced from the country to the towns and cities, and from the community and household economy to the economy of waged labor in production centers (shops and factories) with their own individuality and location and of a supra-human and supra-local scale of socialization (cf. Hobsbawn 1962; cf. Thompson 1963). For wage-earners home may be a haven, a place of rest, convenience, or even self-aggrandizement after a day of obligation, schedule, unchosen tasks, and humiliation. For the houseworker, home is both a work place and a setting for the special though problematic shared pleasures of relatively permanent affiliation. It is clear that these perspectives, qualified as they are by the contradictions of even this bit of unity, are not necessarily compatible even when they coexist in a single individual who works both outside and in the home.

Moreover, housework occurs in relative privacy, while waged work takes place in public places. The wage-earner is, paradoxically, less exposed to the feelings and perceptions of others than the houseworker. Others' impressions of one are more easily managed in public places than in the socially more dense and personally more violative (and therefore contradictory) environment of the home (cf. Goffman 1963). The houseworker has few secrets and cannot easily control how he or she is seen and judged by other family members (cf. Goffman 1961a). Relative privacy of work does not necessarily entail privacy for the worker.

One consequence of these differences is what many husbands and wives report as a "failure of communication," a "lack of understanding," or an inability to find areas of common concern and pleasure (cf. Rubin 1978). Another is the reinforcement of oppressive gender and age-based practices.

Family, community, and culture are enormously problematic under capitalism in ways that are unique because of the domination of society by capital. On the one hand, they provide a degree of stability and interpersonal relevance for individuals that are otherwise unobtainable. On the other hand, capitalist relations of production compromise their social development and finally undermine them. Regardless, they provide foci of ideological deception and control: the proponents of capitalism often claim that "free enterprise" preserves and encourages the "basic values" of home and community. But it should be clear by now that the best it can do is preserve them as obligations made oppressive by the diminishing possibilities of fulfilling them. It should also be clear that the significance of family, community, and culture varies with the sociopolitical development of labor as an historical force and that they have often and under specific circumstances served as issues vital to that development.

CLASS STRUGGLE: RESISTANCE AND REVOLUTION

The subjective aspects of exploitation seem to suggest that radical politics or revolutionary action depend on the development of a political consciousness in immediate regard to exploitation as a feature of the fundamental contradiction of capital and society. Here, "revolutionary action" is intended to mean all the collective activity that could be part of the history of a particular class confrontation; and "consciousness" is used in its psychological rather than sociological sense, as something in individuals that makes them similarly disposed and similarly self-aware.

There are several problems with this reductive overemphasis on subjectivity: 1. revolutionary action in the sense of organized conflict is entirely too limiting a concept for an historical account of social change. The resistance of people to either oppressive or exploitative circumstances may or may not be "revolutionary," and may or may not be accompanied by an awareness of the sort associated with intense and radical political mobilization. In fact, it is theoretically more important to explain the aspects of class struggle that are independent of direct confrontation than the rare, unpredictable, and typically indecipherable moments of revolution, since the former correspond to the internal dialectic of production made explicit in the critique of capital while the latter are contingent on events for which that dialectic can provide only parameters. This shifts attention from the subjective to the objective aspects of revolutionary movement and to the *intrinsically* revolutionary character of capitalism; and it directs theory toward historical dynamics rather than the conjunctural matters that necessarily occupy parties to specific confrontations.[2]

2. The term "consciousness," used in its psychological sense, suggests too great a similarity among people in their orientation to distant ends (instrumentalism), a summing of individuals as in an assembly rather than a composition of collective action as in an ensemble, and identities of mind and experience that could not conceivably be accounted for by the volatility of capitalist development. An account of revolution must conform to a definite logic in the relation of subjective and objective conditions if it is to do more than say that societies change and that they change when people are ready. The subjective aspect of a situation constituted in social relations refers to that situation as if it were being intended, that is to say as dynamic rather than static and with the dynamism of an action rather than a mecha-

nism or natural force. Its objective aspect refers to the situation as if the intention that virtually unifies it in practice is an accomplished fact. This dialectic of subjectivity and objectivity, agency and dynamism, is what gives analysis its historical dimension. It is what makes it possible to have a theory of revolution that is more than narrative accounts of specific revolutions or predictions of specific revolutionary moments and that is part of an authentic political sociology.

The analysis of exploitation and the discussion of some of its ramifications raise what is possibly the key question for Marxian political sociology: under what conditions will the overriding class interest of workers become the basis of a socialist movement aimed at replacing the exploitative division of labor by a new social control of established social production (cf. Laclau and Mouffe 1985, for an attempt to "deconstruct" the authority of this question.) Research has dealt with the composition of and divisions within the working class, the types of association that have bridged those divisions, the actions of unions and parties in regard to different groups of workers (men, women; white, black; national, foreign; industrial, white collar; manual, intellectual; and so on), and the influence of parties, unions, public opinion, and local political movements on working class militancy and solidarity (cf. the journal *KapitaliState;* Kornblum 1974; Aronowitz 1983; Gordon et al. 1982a; Gordon et al. 1982b; Montgomery 1979).

Marxian theory has addressed the relevance of this research to the critique of capitalism, emphasizing in particular the role of communication and education in translating class interest into class politics, and the discursive and group processes implicit in capitalist social relations. For this, it has drawn on many fields of inquiry not ordinarily associated with political economy and not specifically identified as Marxian. This raises questions about the relevance of the non-Marxian disciplines to the socialist movement and its theory, and the meanings of scientifically ambiguous terms, such as "consciousness" and "organization," that are increasingly used by some Marxian theorists to discuss the possibilities and prospects of socialism (cf. Wright 1978; Williams 1977; Eagleton 1983; Jameson 1981; Anderson 1976).

The fact that exploitation and the socialist movement are historical processes that correspond to immediate and local conditions constrained by the overall political economy of capitalism requires that sociologists deal with the historical complexity of the politics of class and the various levels of analysis at which it is theorized. Two aspects have been studied in detail: 1. unity and conflict in the political expression of labor's interest; and 2. changes in the character of class conflict through different periods of capitalist development, with particular attention to the problems of composition and the dialectics of hegemony.

Research on the first aspect has concentrated on the "mystification" of capitalist relations of production within the media, and the relation of class consciousness, however composed, to the uneven development of and therefore the social diversity within capitalism. Research on the second aspect has focussed on the ways in which people have resisted exploitation under the changing conditions of capitalist production and on the experience of class-representative associations such as unions, parties, and radical organizations that operate at the intersection of economics, politics, and daily life (cf. Hobsbawm 1973; cf., for reviews, Ollman and Vernoff 1982, 1984).

The most relevant disciplines have been the history and sociology of labor, "people's history," economic history, the sociology of communication, and the history of economic analysis. Current studies in literary theory are pertinent to all of these though they have not yet assimilated the socio-economic implications of the corresponding disciplines (cf. Eagleton 1983; Jameson 1981; Wiliams 1977; Ollman and Vernoff 1982, 1984; and cf. the journal, *Social Text*).

These disciplines trace the ways in which people have understood their situations, acted jointly on that understanding, and responded to countervailing forces and ideologies. Their critical convergence reminds us that capitalism is and has been a violent and revolutionary movement, that it has enslaved some and freed others, that the working class was created as much by force and guile as economic necessity, that capitalist governments have never represented the working class as such, that workers have always resisted exploitation, that the most vaunted values—in art, religion, and morality—have had strong ideological components, and that the history of capitalism is not simply one of human progress or the triumph of reason and democracy but the history of class struggle.

A review of the ground already covered reveals several sources of the mystification of capitalist social relations. Among these are 1. the wage relation that disguises the gift (surplus value) given by labor to capital, as if the wage were compensation for the total productive effort of the worker rather than a minimum cost to the capitalist of getting unpaid labor; 2. the appearance of logical necessity or natural process in the subordination of workers to machinery, the separation of their work from socially valid purposes, and the requirement that they compete for increasingly deskilled jobs (though such jobs may require training); 3. the consolidation of working class organizations (such as unions) through collective bargaining and legal process around specific issues that concern only segments of the working population; 4. the relation of the concentration and centralization of the means of production to the means and content of public communication; and 5. the unsettling dependence of labor on the uncertain value of the money paid as wage.

Each of these poses problems for class consciousness, and therefore for effective opposition to capital.

CLASS STRUGGLE AND CAPITALIST PRODUCTION

Class struggle is, on the other hand, more than the history of the socialist movement and its moments of mobilization and confrontation. The opposition of classes and the contradiction of economy and society are intrinsic properties of capitalist production, features of its very possibility as a mode of production (cf. Ollman and Vernoff 1982, 1984, for reviews of the various disciplines). This will become clearer in the following discussions of the relation of knowledge to production and of the ways in which the antagonism inherent in the social relations of production is a constitutive feature of society and everyday life.

The analysis of capitalist production suggests that prevailing conceptions of productivity are entirely too abstract to be appropriate to an understanding of any particular historical situation (cf. Ecker, 1983), and in any case rely on a notion of usefulness of the product that is inconsistent with its character as a commodity, an object produced solely for sale. These points require a reevaluation of what has occasionally been said to be an unreasoning hostility of workers toward intellectuals, science, and scientific methods (a variant of the argument that only tradition opposes "modernization").

The meaning of "productivity" depends upon the type of economy to which the term is applied. For capitalism, where wealth consists of a surplus extracted from the activity of a total class (labor) and used by those who own it in ways that affect but cannot be influenced by that class, the "productivity" of labor as an economic concept refers to a measurable increase from one period to another of that portion of surplus value that is controlled by capital. It does not refer to the number of goods produced or the degree to which social needs are satisfied, though these are often taken to be implicit in it. As an economic concept, "productivity" entails an actively expropriative antagonism of capital toward the society of producers on which it depends. This implies that advances in management and technology do not necessarily serve the interest of society, and in any case must be evaluated in terms of the particular interest—capital—that defines that significance.

It follows that knowledge in its relation to techniques for increasing the productivity of labor cannot be considered neutral or universally valid. Because of the extent and intensiveness of capital's influence, it also follows that it is difficult if not impossible to distinguish basic from applied knowledge or technique (cf. Habermas 1970a, 1975; Braverman 1975; Ecker 1983).

The ordinary uses of the terms "productivity" and "knowledge" disguise the class interest that determines their significance as concepts linking theory and practice. As such, they suggest that any resistance to the expansion of capital is irrational, unfair, or inconsistent with social progress, and that hostility to the implementation of economically relevant knowledge expresses ignorance, prejudice, or superstition. In a society divided by the class division of production, however, the relation of knowledge to interest is a condition of any theory of knowledge that attempts to account for intellectual practices, results, divergencies, and development. Furthermore, where the class division is rationalized, as it must be, by considerations of productivity rationalized in turn as profit, one cannot deny at least the possibility that hostility to the processes and results of intellectual work is both strategically necessary and intellectually valid. Indeed, to deny that possibility is to deny the existence and/or conceivability of capitalism as a society-constituting mode of production.

This brings us back to the radically antagonistic relationship of capital and society and the incompatible perspectives that correspond to it. The critique of capital shows that the class antagonism is a permanent, original, and intensive feature of the capitalist division of production. The operations of capitalist production consist of capital (direction and control accountable to the private accumulation of wealth) and labor (socialized activity mobilized solely in the interest of capital). These operations account for capitalist production in detail as well as at the limits of its national and global economies. The antagonism is characteristic of and implicit in every activity that bears on the production, circulation, and accumulation of capitalist wealth.

Capital expands only if labor (as society) experiences a loss, and because the mode of production necessarily includes both aspects, labor's loss is also finally capital's. Profit in general requires a constant increase in the general level of exploitation; without that, capital as a whole ceases to function economically. The conditions of labor in general improve only at capital's expense. Therefore capitalist productivity requires control of labor within the process of production itself in regard to the sociality of work, the technical relations of mechanism and routine, and the task-practical relations of decision and performance. Yet it requires precisely the social facilitation of performance, flexibility of effort, and responsiveness to unanticipated problems that these moments of control would deny.

It follows that the benefits of capitalist management are not only antipathetic to the interest of society but only short run and sectoral.

Either the human component of production is suppressed and capital in general fails, or it is expanded and private ownership gives way to the social control of production. In any case, because it depends on socialized labor, capitalist production reinforces the opposing tendencies of cooperation and suppression or containment. Thus, the progress of the society of producers within capitalist relations of production, and as either capital's facility or the socialist movement, consists as much of resistance as cooperation. In fact resistance to as well as cooperation in production serve both the particular interest of capital and the general interest of society, but only the latter can assert itself in the long run as a continuing base of self-reproducing society.

It follows also that the confrontation of labor and capital is internal to the capitalist mode of production. It does not reflect differences of attitude, inevitable technical problems of rational coordination, or the scarcities of nature; nor can it be understood as an instance of social conflict (organizations competing for resources) that lends itself to institutional compromise (Poulantzas 1975a, 1975b). Indeed, attempts to qualify the interest of either class eventually leads to struggles against compromise itself (cf. Davis 1980a; Mandel 1980).

If we look at this antagonism from the standpoint of capitalist society as a whole, capital's side of the class struggle involves 1. a constant effort to remake the instruments of production in order continually to shift control from labor to management and from people to equipment, thereby continuing the process of abstracting labor—that is, reproducing labor power; 2. the development of legal mechanisms that increase the mobility and decrease the risks of private property and therefore reinforce the class domination of society; 3. the continual enforcement of competition among workers, thereby cheapening the general wage; 4. the reinforcement of state policies that free capital from any obligation to the society of producers that makes capitalist production possible; 5. the use of coercion and ideological manipulation to suppress social aspirations, undermine working class associations (unions, parties and so on), and dampen the spirit and practice of resistance; 6. the conquest of foreign populations through force or by fiscal threat and manipulation in order to ensure cheap labor and/or an expanding market, and in order to contain resistance as much as possible on a global scale.

Labor's struggle consists of every act that simultaneously interferes with capital's appropriation of the surplus and contributes to the political unity of the working class both within and across national boundaries. This has included, at various times and in various places, sabotage, slow-downs, sit-ins, strikes, and insurrection. It has also included the formation of unions and left parties, political compromises in which segments of labor have offered a degree of orderliness in the affairs of industry in exchange for some measure of political power within the state, and more inchoate forms of resistance that involve absenteeism, voluntary turnover, and the sharing of complaints such that a texture of protest is established with or without the instruments of its realization.

Class struggle does not then refer simply to the confrontation of groups—that is, insurrection, rebellion, or revolution. It refers to the normal interaction of the principles of production under capital. It is an inevitable feature of the exploitative use of social labor as such and therefore appears in every process identifiable within the framework of capitalist economy. Resistance is a feature of exploitation, not merely its accompaniment or something introduced as a reaction or response. Our discussion of the separation of purpose and activity, above, points toward a further understanding of the internally contradictory character of all action that expresses that separation. Each moment of a job, each task, each directed movement of the body, each choice, is inherently ambivalent because 1. the separation of those moments from the purposes that animate them leaves the actor uncertain as to why he or she is acting—spontaneously and for purposes that express experience, or because of a purpose imposed by some other external agency; 2. from the perspective of the act whose purpose is external to the worker, activity can only be felt as automatic, a feature of role, or a technical obligation to the mechanisms of production. The result is an inherent and constantly registered ambivalence within action itself (cf. Blum and McHugh 1984; LeFebvre 1971). Freud made this theoretically explicit by showing how every act registers in one way or another the ambiguity of need and choice; Marxism establishes the historical conditions under which this is generally the case and the philosophical conditions in terms of which it is necessarily or analytically true.

Thus, at one limit resistance is traceable to the class dimension of capitalist production and revealed in the ambivalence of the agent, whether verbally articulated or not. At this limit, resistance is neither fully self-conscious nor guided by deliberation. At the opposite limit, resistance is undertaken beyond the immediate technical situation of work, in the sociality of workers or in class-representative politics. There, it is deliberately poised against an enemy, and the politics of class struggle is the history of the identification of that enemy—the machine, the boss, the organization, the propertied class, the class-state, capital—and the articulation of the relations that make class politics necessary and practical.

Class struggle expresses at all points the fundamental contradiction of capitalist economy and society: the division of production by class is essential to the capitalist economy, but capital can neither coordinate the productive base that it needs nor tolerate the society that is the organizational condition necessary for such coordination. The competitive character of the capitalist market economy ensures as well the uneven development of economically dominated society, an anarchism of priorities disguised as "free competition." Finally, the class division mitigates against generally valid policies even if it were possible to establish a policy composition on the bases of local transactions for immediate profit.

The unity of capitalism, from the perspective either of capital represented by the state or of abstracted labor represented by class associations (unions, parties, and so on), is contingent, fragile, and temporary at best. For capital there is only the appearance of unity; for abstracted labor there is only unity in prospect or an unstable unity of practice. Nevertheless, the overall dynamic of capitalism, its principle of development, is reflected in the general contradiction to which all class-based organization responds, the impossibility of reconciling the social character of production with its character as private property.

SUMMARY

Marx's account of capitalism analyzes the exploitive relations of commodity production, class relations enacted both at the level of the total society and in the immediate situations of production and exchange. Commodity production, exploitation, uneven development, the reconciliation of local transactions with the total dynamic of capitalism, and class struggle can no longer be the separate topics of separate social sciences, but are features of a single, though heterogeneous and complex, reality, the capitalist mode of production. As such, they are objects of a specific and multi-faceted discipline, Marxism. Class conflict is neither something added to nor an exceptional state of the capitalist order. It is intrinsic to the dialectic of the capitalist accumulation of wealth and cannot be wished away, healed by good will or politics alone, or considered to be an inevitable product of human nature that nothing can erase.

Marxian analysis, like psychoanalysis, is not a theory to make people happy, or one to cultivate a taste for wealth or power. Society can no more avoid its troubles than it can its history. People are in the midst of social change at all times. The question is never one of status quo or "what we have" versus the "radicalism of the socialist," but of how to reckon with the extreme and constantly unsettled and unsettling character of capitalist society for all of its people.

In capitalism, issues are joined only through the relative power of the classes. Capitalists have always understood this; labor's understanding has evolved more slowly and, as yet, remains in the process of formation. This is the hardest fact to acknowledge, since the achievement of an historically authentic society, one that emerges from capitalism, depends upon the political mobilization of the working class, at present across as well as within the boundaries of the nation-state. We evade it by indulging nostalgia for formerly integrated social orders, by demanding a policy of total reform as if institutions exist for such an enactment and as if it could in any case avoid the crises it is intended to heal, by trying to establish theories "of the middle" that can appeal to the spirit of compromise when the terms of compromise are yet to be imagined, and by attacking the harbingers of bad news—Marxian analysis and class-based unions, parties, and social movements. We evade it by rewriting history to exclude the history of labor—as the history of technology (a history of things) or the history of democracy and freedom (a history of unhistoricized ideals). Finally, we evade it by absorbing ourselves in the infinite practical elaborations of commodity production and consumption and the various abstract and antihistorical humanisms—religious and utopian—whose increasing preciousness in our culture's propaganda testifies to the harsh and antihuman reality they so often disguise.

It would be wrong to assume from its critical stance that Marxism is merely negative or that Marxists are cynical, or that the Marxian tradition has failed to acknowledge the diversity of consciousness implicit in any full idea of "society" (cf. Bakhtin 1981; Thompson 1963). Marx's recognition of the historical character of capitalism contains a deep appreciation of capital's accomplishments—the vastness of modern production and the socialization of labor as the society of producers. His critique reflects both the revolutionary achievements of capitalism and the human costs of those achievements.

The analysis of capitalism's contradictions suggests that though theory manifests interests it is more than a taking of sides. The analysis of ideology, to be further elaborated upon, suggests that the effects of ideology are due to the fact that the reality of capitalist production is problematic, contradictory, and difficult to penetrate from within the local situations that embody it. Consciousness and theory are themselves historical rather than above or beyond history. It is not surprising, then, that the exploited may from time to time defend as well as attack capital; and even that those who share capital's wealth may occasionally take exception to its principle.

Like any human science, Marxism attempts to explain its phenomenon from whatever perspective provides the greatest integration of material. As a science of capitalist *society,* it must deal with the intentional, and therefore practical, aspect as a level of analysis sufficient to comprehend both the social order of production and its historical dynamic. From this point of view, what is important to theory as, one might say, data, are not the opinions people express from time to time. Certainly, these must be explained, but theory must deal primarily with the subjective aspects of capitalist social relations coordinate with the objective aspects for a given configuration of capitalist development—what those relations are for the practice of making as well as living history.

Notes

1. Sociologists have documented various forms of social differentiation—by gender, market position, ethnicity. But these have been largely examined in abstraction from the mode or modes of production to which they correspond or in which their significance is determined. Concepts such as "status" and "power" have been imposed on what may be far more complex orders of difference in order to provide opportunities for quantification and to establish a trans-historical theoretization of empirical differences. From the standpoint of the critique of ideology, these impositions provide support for particular interests hostile to the universal values of equality and cooperation (cf. Cicourel 1974; Bittner 1965). From the standpoint of epistemology, they evade the question of the historical significance of generalized social divisions. In any case, Marxian theory attempts to establish the general foundation of generalized differentiation in the most general features of capitalism. It follows that not all differentiating criteria are of equal significance, that generalized differentiation is not susceptible to change by strictly cultural or political means, and that changes in patterns of social differentiation are in one way or another tied to conditions of yet more fundamental change. This does not mean that Marxism opposes movements that are not directly opposed to class exploitation but that it evaluates such movements by two criteria: 1. the extent to which their politics reach beyond particular concerns to the most general concerns of society, and 2. the extent to which their critique of the conditions they directly oppose embraces more fundamental conditions. These criteria reflect the fundamental proposition of Marxian theory, that capitalist production exploits society as a whole.

2. It would be arbitrary to draw too fine a distinction between the two since the dialectic of theory itself can only be described in terms of a relation of historical and conjunctural formulations. It is nevertheless important to maintain the distinction for purposes of clarifying the general critique of capital.

8

The Political Dimension of Class Struggle

THE POLITICS OF class struggle have been understood largely in terms of two problems: the first is the class character of the state, and the second is the character of organized resistance and opposition to the exploitative relations of capitalist production.

The first involves description of the historically specific properties of the capitalist state. The French Revolution established popular sovereignty as a principle of political action and analysis; the "industrial revolution" in England inscribed class relations on the national order of society (cf. Hobsbawm 1962). The modern capitalist state bears the burdens and carries the obligations of this "dual revolution" (Miliband 1977).

The state institutes legal limits to democracy that systematically ratify and legitimize the expansion of capital at the expense of labor. Through its function as bank of last and occasionally even first resort, it sustains the price-making money market; and it attempts to manage the class struggle by means of its monopoly on the instruments of violence and its partial control of the mass media. At the same time, the centralization of fiscal policy allows the state to stratify and, to the extent possible, coordinate the various fractions of capital (cf. Miliband 1977; Moffit 1983; Wolfe 1977; O'Connor 1973; Offe 1971; and cf. the journal *KapitaliState*).

The state can perform these tasks insofar as there are mechanisms for maintaining its identity, organizational quality, and capacity to grow in relation to the problems posed by the class struggle, the uneven expansion of capital, and the challenge of both to the political boundaries in which those mechanisms are made legitimate. Aside from its class basis, the dilemmas of state policy reflect the fact that the organizational stability and relative autonomy the state requires to perform its immediate tasks do not permit it sufficient flexibility to operate in regard to the contradictions of capitalist production as such—that is, to operate as a transformative agency even if political power is not superceded by capitalist economy (cf. Miliband 1977).

Other problems arise in connection with the difficulties of making exploitation legitimate to those who are exploited without the use of explicit antidemocratic propaganda: managing the value of national money in a speculative and militarized global economy, sustaining the univocal dominance of a capitalist interest against its own internal intraclass divisions and against the potential political force of labor, and maintaining the state's own fiscal viability without undermining investment in commodity production (cf. Wallerstein 1974; O'Connor 1973; Offe 1971; Jessop 1982; Aglietta 1979).

Marxian theories of the state have attempted 1. to conceptualize its class character in a way that is compatible with the tendencies toward relative autonomy and organizational coherence necessary for it to fulfill its tasks; and 2. to establish the relationship between the economic conditions of state action and the state's pervasive social presence and cultural impact.

The programmatic statement remains that of Marx and Engels in *The Communist Manifesto* about the political development of the property-owning class, the "bourgeoisie:"

> Each step in the development of the bourgeoisie was accompanied by a corresponding political advance of that class. An oppressed class under the sway of the feudal nobility, an armed and self-governing association in the medieval commune, here independent urban republic. . . . , there taxable "third estate" of the monarchy . . . , afterwards in the period of manufacture proper, serving either the semi-feudal or the absolute monarchy as a counterpoise against the nobility and, in fact, cornerstone of the great monarchies in general, the bourgeoisie has at last, since the establishment of modern industry and of the world market, conquered for itself, in the modern representative State, exclusive political sway. The executive of the modern State is but a committee for managing the common affairs of the whole bourgeoisie [1948].

The point is not that the capitalist state is a tool utterly controlled by the capitalist class, but that it has properties of agency that respond in the fashion of mediation to the overall needs of that class, and not on command but as all that it can do (Miliband 1969, 1977; Poulantzas, 1978). It is important to remember that the term "class" does not signify a portion of the population but an operation within the capitalist division of production. The state taken as government represents a portion of the population in terms of the interest of capital, which is to say the practice of capitalist production as such. It follows that studies of policy biases toward one or another fraction of the property-owning segment of the population can only provide a rough indication of the nature of the capitalist state (cf. Wolfe 1973, 1977).

It is all too easy to confuse the actual constituency of the state (capital) with the apparent constituency (portions of the population able to exercise pressure on state agencies and overall policy). When this occurs, conclusions are likely to be drawn about politics—that it should orient toward the building of constituencies in the latter sense—that are inconsistent with what we know to be the limitations of the state as an instrumentality for socializing property.

Still, it is possible, again roughly, to indicate the state's bias by noting how policy is implemented—through the private or corporate sector—and financed—by resources controlled by capital in its most concentrated form. Empirical studies of the distribution of power within the national population are, as indicated above, merely an indication of how power is determined within capitalist production. While there is no question that economically dominant groups tend to be most active in government, most involved in selecting top personnel in government agencies and its executive branch, and most influential in the determination of state policy (cf. Domhoff 1967; Miliband 1969; Mills 1956), it is nevertheless the case that the composition of a class interest for capital by the state may undermine the power and influence of those fractions. The reproduction of capital does not depend upon the preservation of particular interests of particular sectors of the population but upon policies aimed at dealing with the contradictions of capitalist production—in the commodity, within money, between price and value, between labor and capital, between production and the market, and between the society of producers and the private and localized disposition of social resources.

It may very well be that a thorough analysis of the state would demonstrate its difference from government and define it in relation to the agencies of capital. Early Marxian theories of law suggested that the corporate form of enterprise itself provides the forms of reproduction necessary to account for all the facts that presumably must be accounted for by a theory of the state (Renner, 1949). In any case, the empirical research is suggestive, though it cannot alone explicate the nature of class bias in the state if only because that bias cannot depend simply on who runs its chief sections or who is temporarily in command of its executive. The bias must be theorized; as such, it has to do with the peculiar dependence of state functions on the steady expansion of capital if they are to be carried out as consistently as possible within the imperatives of capitalist production. The state can only operate if its activities are compatible with the overall expansiveness of capital, and events suggest that this is a more serious limitation then we had believed.

On the other hand, given its virtual presence amidst capital's contradictions, it ought to be clear that the state cannot be immune from the influence of labor. Since an adequate composition of capital depends on some degree of support for the society of producers, states must develop policies that provide at least minimally for that society, regardless of the ideologies or intentions of those who control state agencies. A failure to do so would inevitably lead to a decay of the integrative resources on which socialized labor must depend—transportation, schooling, housing, and the rest. This by itself does not mean that state policies might not violate those conditions (cf. Offe, 1971). What it does imply is that policies that are inconsistent with the basic needs of the society of producers will exacerbate the crisis of capital beyond the state's capacity to support the class relation other than by intimidation and brutality. Any other course would lead to an abandonment of the terrain those policies presume to protect and therefore to a systematic transformation of the relation of state and society.

From the point of view of practice, whether or not and to what degree labor's interest influences state policies depends upon the momentary articulation of that interest, the sanctions that can be exercised by unions, parties, and other working class formations, and the solidarity and discipline that characterizes their popular mobilization (cf. Piven and Cloward 1982; Brown and Goldin 1973; Blackburn 1978). This raises two issues of decisive significance to political sociology: the role of unions and parties in the political life of capitalist nations, and the conditions under which the working class is able to press for socialist reforms and ultimately socialism (Gorz 1967, 1976; Gordon et al. 1982a; Aronowitz 1973, 1983; Poulantzas 1975b).

Again, practical considerations have dominated research. The result is an accumulation of empirical findings and little solid conceptualization. Regardless of this, it seems fairly well agreed that political sociology must do more than list the practical conditions of confrontation; it must demonstrate the existence of an underlying texture of resistance that corresponds to capitalism's historical dynamic and thereby makes it possible to conceive of and observe the course of political development (cf. Thompson 1963, 1975; Brown and Goldin 1973; Willis 1977). This requires both a documentation of activities that clearly oppose capital's interest and an interpretation of subtle and often inarticulate conduct in terms of its relation to mobilization and resistance, including what is often referred to as "working class culture" (cf. Williams 1977; Aronowitz 1973; Thompson 1978; Eagleton 1983; Jameson 1981; Jones 1971).

The main topics of Marxian scholarship on resistance have referred primarily to specific moments of revolutionary confrontation. The analysis suggests, however, that the most important topic is precisely this underlife of protest, as E. P. Thompson's work has made abundantly clear (cf. also Goffman 1961). The reason is that "class struggle" refers to more than momentary confrontation; it is, as noted in the last chapter, a conceptualization of capitalist relations in all their extent and possible detail. This is why there has been so much recent interest among Marxian scholars in the sociologies of everyday life that emphasize "praxis," discourse, and meaning (cf. Garfinkel 1967; Goffman 1974; Habermas 1970b, 1979). Studies of conversation, the process of gestural exchange, and the movement of signs in weakly bounded and highly mediated discourses offer methodologies that go far beyond the standard empirical methods in identifying the texture of resistance, the infraprocesses without which class politics (and the society of the producers) in any form is virtually incomprehensible (cf. Thompson 1975, for an interesting example of this turn in methodology; and cf. Brown 1983–84).

The non-Marxian sociologies have been unable to explain social movements and protest without reducing them either to the psychology of their participants, the irrationalities of unrationalized collectivism, or relatively simplistic models of instrumental action, or employing the dei ex machina of systems analysis paradoxically to explain what the idea of system seems to exclude (cf. Brown and Goldin 1973). Typical accounts refer to exceptional or external conditions (system strain, the breakdown of norms, deprivation, agitation, and so on) that disturb conventional or established patterns of conduct (cf. Smelser 1963; Turner 1964; Tilly 1978; Gurr 1969); at that point action is said to become momentarily disorganized, spontaneous, volatile, and subject either to primitive or over-rationalized processes of coordination. It is presumed that the normal state of affairs is a unity relatively free of conflict, a condition, to be sure, of vulnerability to structurally specific extra-systemic factors, but one that is not possible in the capitalist mode of production and its society.

Other theorists of social movements and collective behavior have emphasized the rationality of needs underlying particular protest activities, and therefore the need to explore the build-up, forms, and internal organization of collective action as reflections of the underlying rationality or self-regulation of need (cf. Tilly 1978). Regardless of this refinement, it is clear that a theory of collective behavior is possible as part of a general social theory only if conflict is taken as an essential feature of rather than separate from the normal state of affairs, and only if conflict is conceived of in a sufficiently fundamental way to explain both ordinary and extraordinary action (riots, protests, insurrections, and revolutions). This is why the demonstration that there is disorder and conflict at the heart of the capitalist formation is so significant a contribution of Marxian analysis to political sociology. Capitalism is not and could not be a balanced and complete system of orderly relations of tasks, institutions, and people. It operates as a contradiction of mutually necessary operations whose opposition is the historical condition of what we call capitalist development. This, in turn, is one reason why Marxism does not conceive of socialism as a catastrophic change but as a deepening and integration of the historical accomplishment of capital: socialism is already prepared in the body of capitalist relations.[1]

SUMMARY

The Marxian theory of revolution does not simply collect, review, and generalize from empirical cases of exceptional action against the state. Its primary concern is the *development* of class struggle in relation to the contradictions of capitalism. It encompasses both a great deal of what has in traditional sociological texts been called "collective behavior," and the whole range of activities shown by symbolic interactionist and ethnomethological studies to involve attempts by groups to resolve the unresolvable, reconcile what cannot be reconciled, reproduce what has already irrevocably changed, and institute and reinstitute the interactive and intersubjective aspects of life under even the most alienating of conditions.

The following chapters introduce some ares of study that extend Marxian sociology beyond the stricter limits of the critique of political economy that is its most rigorous tradition. While these will be somewhat speculative, they should be read as an attempt to bring those areas into line with the critique of capital. Some of these topics have already been discussed above in connection with specific problem areas. But since their literature is now sufficiently developed for them to be taken as sociologies of topics organized loosely around an empirical or conceptual paradigm, it seems legitimate to speculate about them from the standpoint of the critique that generates the problems that make them sociologically significant. The focus of the next chapters is the complex of topics variously referred to as ideology, culture, and consciousness. The discussion attempts to bring these adjacent literatures to bear on Marxian theory and to show the latter's bearing on their historical significance. (cf. Eagleton 1983; Williams 1980; Brown 1983–84).

Note

1. What have been called "commodity riots" are not, in this account, reactions to deprivation but generalized responses, collectively instituted, to the contradiction between the society of producers and private ownership. Maldistribution is experienced in the riot as an inevitable feature of private control and the expropriation of the surplus by a privileged class. When official control appears at the same time to be weak, power shifts not to individuals who are now free to act as they please, but to individuals as members of and therefore subject to collectivity. The weakening of official power is a sign of opposing forces, class-based or only vaguely class-oriented, and not simply as an opening for individual expressiveness, as was claimed by older theories of "crowds" (cf. Brown and Goldin, 1973, for a more elaborate theoretical presentation of aspects of this position and critique of its alternatives).

9

Ideology, Culture, Consciousness

THE MARXIAN LITERATURE lists at least two pervasive sources of ideology in capitalist society. *First, the fact that the capitalist political economy defines and therefore can be said to operate hegemonically across the entire terrain of economically relevant and economically dependent social life makes it difficult to speak sensibly in ways that are inconsistent with it.* Representations, figures of speech, likely topics of interaction, and received discourses find their thematic ground and rhetorical plausibility in connection with the theoretically identified practical antinomies of commodity production: the disjunctions of purpose and activity, exchange and use, the currency of evaluation and socially significant value, the momentary event and extended context, arrangement and history, productivity and affection, work and leisure, thing and person, and economy and society.

Similarly, the ambiguities of "freedom," "moral obligation," "creativity," and "taste" provide frames within which literature and discourse find their special fluencies. The virtual totalization of society by capital breeds as well its own version of a curious reversal, an intellectual totalization of others. It requires, first, the assignment, invention, or use of points of absolute difference from another so that society can be displayed, despite itself, as a unity of interest with the right of self-identification. Second, this absolutely foreign otherness to society takes the form of something complete, permanently disposed and therefore incapable of learning (and, it follows, without the right of self-identification), identical with its name, and utterly external. Indeed, that category, familiar in the related discourses of patriotism, ethnocentrism, and racism, constantly threatens to absorb all that is even momentarily foreign to capitalism and its ideologies—as when union struggles at the end of the nineteenth century were characterized as the work of foreign elements come to "communalize" American workers, or contemporary anti-capitalist revolutions appear to threaten society itself with, as Henry Kissinger once put it, "too much democracy."[1]

But it would be an error to assume that the category of this "foreignness" is merely a contrivance of propagandists. It completes the idealization of a unity constantly threatened by its own internal divisions and therefore a source of constant confusion and even despair. By imposing an equally idealized unity of otherness—an absolute negativity—on whatever falls outside of the legitimate frames of discourse and the practices of and adjuncts to capitalism, we allow ourselves to read those protests, assertions of sociality, and struggles for survival in a mood of defensive cyncism and contempt, or with condescension and a military-like detachment from the lives that they signify. The idealized unity of "the other" becomes a kind of abstract scapegoat, or a mythic figure, on which, without risk, we enact our own futility, frustration, sense of betrayal, helplessness, and subjection; and it is more often than not depicted as so utterly strange that it appears as a *total* ordering of will, judgment, and hostile determination: witness references in political speeches and in journalistic commentary to "Marxist societies," "totalitarianism," "the rest of the world," and so on (cf. Barthes 1972).

At the extreme, in its current form, is the image of totalitarianism, a term that moralizes that otherness and compresses into it all that could be manifest as fixed and beyond history and humanity. The image of a total domination, a perfect repression, a humanity lost to imposed unities and foreign purposes—all of this stands as an opposition to "the free world," which in turn requires more and more elaborate absolute representations on its own account—religious, nationalistic, missionary.

Like most mythologies, however, this merely reverses what is most intolerable about the socioeconomic order of power and need that it defends, neutralizing criticism from within even as it denies the validity of criticism from without. This is the sort of displacement that limits the critical disposition in literature and the discourses of the social sciences, as it does politics and daily life, to the normative promotion of the logic of capitalist accumulation ("freedom" to exchange) even as the contradictions of capital become more and more apparent. Anticommunism takes its intellectual force from this displacement and in turn operates upon the culture that originally affirms it (cf. Wolfe 1973; Rogin 1967; Miliband, et al. 1984; and cf. Said's related discussion, 1977). Thus, anticommunism, probably the oldest explicitly capitalist ideology, becomes one of the most fundamental constraints on modern critical thought, writing, and speaking. Once unleashed, its absolutism threatens to challenge even the rational boundaries and limited humanism of the culture and mode of production it defends.

Second, the creativity of daily life requires an ease of interaction, a secured sense of continuity and familiarity, that is not possible in the midst of the contraditions of capitalist production and the abstractions of its market. This moral vacuum, so well described by Erving Goffman (1963), is filled (fills itself) with discursive intervals, covered lapses, that allow speech to take any turn the needs of publicity find convenient or might require and that are signified as interconnections among ideas that are as arbitrary as the relations of commodities (cf. Garfinkel 1967). The discursive chaining of signs regardless of intention to signify resembles the fluency imposed by the capitalist market on the circulation of goods, money, and people: motion without rest, a permanent mobilization perpetually available for purposes yet and always unannounced (cf. Habermas 1970b; Foucault 1973; Brown 1983–84).

The coherence of such a "semiosis" relies on centering myths of self and other that replace concepts, ideas, and practical referents as occasions for continuing speech.Given the restrictions of life that are determined by capital, it is not surprising that those centering myths are key figures at the points of propaganda's greatest fluency: "movements," "flows," "investments," "exchanges," "decisions," "policies," "systems," "national security interests," and all the other cultural effulgences that reflect the opposition of capitalist rationalization to society and history.

The comprehensiveness of capitalist production, and the inevitable moral vacuum in the local settings it inevitably leaves behind, are findings of the Marxian critique of ideology. However, they suggest a degree of domination that is not consistent with the results of the more general critique of capital. The first thesis, the cultural hegemony of capital, is often argued as if there is an unopposed tendency for capitalism to extend the form of its immediate product, the commodity, without limit throughout the various spheres of society. This is a useful though limited abstraction. If the "profit motive" tends to make everything vulnerable to the contradictory logic of evaluation and exchange (if everything comes to have a "price" that ultimately fails to represent the difference it makes to society, and if that vulnerability enforces a valuational scheme that presupposes but dispossesses potentially meaningful effort, then the steady conversion of all things to the commodity form entails their quantitative standardization and their irreducible connection with exploitative social relations.

This cultural movement of the commodity form beyond commodity production is said to occur through a market-induced extension of production itself. This is precisely the reverse of the process by which capitalist production normally expands: here, the controlling factor is price or some analogy to it; there, it was value. The difference is certainly important for understanding the problems created by the extension of the commodity form to other "forms" initially not produced by labor power for the accumulation of wealth, notably the difficulty of determining meaning or significance (cf. Offe 1971). But for the study of ideology it is sufficient to note the virtual *but never actual* universalization of the logic of exchange and exploitation and its influence on but not total control of representations, figures of thought and speech, and discourses. In this, all things, human and nonhuman, appear *in part* as commodities, subject to infinite comparability; and all significant social relations appear *in part* as relations among things that can only be imposed on people but not be willed by them as an ensemble of their own mutually oriented activities.

Marx referred to these appearances in his initial abstraction of universal exchange as consequences of a "fetishization" of commodities. At its extreme limit, things acquire a higher reality and greater moral worth than people, whose only "value" lies in those properties that make them comparable to things or to each other taken as things.

On the other hand, the second thesis, the moral vacuum, is a more dramatic and accessible topic for analysis even though its content is more variable, consisting as it does of proliferating materials geared to particular moments in which the mobilization of people has become an issue. Here, we are dealing with the generation of familiar ideological matter in the mass media, within educational establishments, and through the mediation of special occasions that constitute, periodically and as if at moments of crisis, a fully articulate but asocial "public sphere." This familiar matter—familiar because always formulaic and immediately derivative—is reconstructed in various media as the stuff of slogan, myth, tale, and legend, and with a narrowing frame that restricts the possibilities of critical reflection (cf. Dahlgren 1977; Ewen, 1976; Barthes 1972; Gitlin 1980; Horkheimer and Adorno 1972). The narrowness of the frame is, from the standpoint of form, a result of the extreme stylization of material, its abstraction from context, the episodic manner of its presentation, and the conventional formalities of the occasions of its appearance—in "news," at school, on television, in speeches, and so on—that neutralize the impact of its content.

There is an immense literature that traces the history of specific ideological forms, their characteristic types of display, the occasions of their presentation, their sociological origins, their institutional quality, and the contradictions of their impact (cf. Mattelart 1980; Schiller 1971; Ewen 1976; Wolfe 1973; Marcuse 1964). It suggests above all that capital—its principle of economy—has established the types of media and public discourse that it needs or that at least serve its convenience. It does not, however, imply that there is a single ideology, unopposed "hegemony," or coherence of representation (cf. *Working Papers in Cultural Studies,* 10, 1977; Jameson 1981; Althusser 1971; Williams 1977).

MEDIA: REITERATIVE AND NONREITERATIVE

If one moves through that history from the individually to the socially consumed media, from printed and bound messages to unbound and invasive electronic productions, it is possible to see important changes in communicative discretion and disposition (cf. Brown 1983–84; Eagleton 1983; Williams 1960, 1961; Burke 1978; Bakhtin 1968): 1. the electronic media, particularly radio and television, provide material that accumulates in relation to its "reception" in such a way that the order of that accumulation can neither be discerned as such nor repeated. We can call such media *nonreiterative* (Brown 1983–84). By contrast, a book can be reread, and the succession of its rereadings take on the formal properties of successive approximations of a "structure:" this because it (a) is portable in the most individualistic sense of the term—it has definite space-time coordinates and can be absolutely possessed; (b) it is physically self-contained by virtue of the conventions governing the "reception" of bound and paginated matter; (c) it is totally available at an instant and therefore capable of circulating intact without losing its identity and of being read independently of contextual constraints on reading as such; (d) it can be addressed without explicit reference to any content-forming context, and thus can be taken as an object in the service of commentary—because it is a commodity in fact, because of the conventions that attach to its completed physicality, and because of its endless accessibility and duplicatability. Moreover, these properties, taken together, enforce a constant recapitulation of material, taken in the course of that recapitulation, as content; this, in turn, reinforces those conventions that give recapitulation its general form that in turn makes possible any specific recapitulation (cf. Brown 1983–84; Eagleton 1983).[?] To read for specific content is to reinforce the totalization, or completion, of what is read and therefore its possible isolation from and loss of reflective relevance to the sphere of practice.

As a result, reading has always been something apart from and in opposition to ordinary conversation and therefore to the immediately historical aspect of sociality (cf. Sartre 1966). In contrast, it is not possible to repeat the "reception" of a broadcast or to listen/view it again without distorting (in the sense of constituting anew) its content. Aural material occurs in an internal and therefore situationally relevant time of "reception," as a sequence of irreversible growth, just as phased visual matter (film). This sequence necessarily—if it is to have internal sense—begins for memory before its own official initiation; it begins in and intrudes upon, one might say, a situation already in process. Furthermore, the circumstances that surround its "reception" indelibly mark its appearance with their own unrepeatability and therefore contribute to its intersection with other projects.

Consequently, electronic media diminish what is called the "message quality" of communicated material, loosen its boundaries and make each item less distinct and less memorable in itself. Left alone, the facts of this unrepeatability and incompleteness bring such communication into line with ordinary discourse (cf. Garfinkel 1967). The only way of managing this so as to reduce its critical potential is to introduce into the aural, visual, or mixed sequence something formulaic that can replace the broadcast as an event with the sense of its having been no more than the condition of a product—for example, a joke, a news item, information, a game, a contest, or a drama (cf. Brown 1983–84). One can study the history of modern broadcasting from the standpoint of exactly this realization, the development of a form of broadcast intended to elide its own character as a problematic relation of intention and realization, situation and object, and as an event that cannot reiterate itself and therefore cannot have fully controlled effects. Such a study would include a domestic ecology of media use, an analysis of the situation in which "reception" occurs, which would show unequivocally the limits of deception, manipulation, and control in practical circumstances (everyday life) that cannot evade at least some self-critical reference to context. (Bakhtin 1968).

2. Radio and television broadcasts are consumed collectively and impose an ecology upon the normally domestic scenes of their consumption. Even in bars and other public places the scene is domestic, involving suspensions of the anti-intimacies of the controlled work place and the "public sphere" of opinion. These media are, perhaps more than electronic and in addition to being nonreiterative, social media; the home computer, in many of its uses, is merely an extension that highlights the fact. They have something in common with the oldest and most popular forms of art (cf. Bakhtin 1968). As a consequence, their effects depend upon and are qualified by the relatively uncontrolled discourses that accompany the "reception" of their material; and those discourses are mixed and intermingled in such a way that no speaker can or has fully to account for what is spoken.[3]

We "watch" television only by appropriating what we see and hear to what we are doing with others. Groups, not individuals, are the elemental viewers and listeners to the new social media (cf. Brown 1983; 1985). The result for these viewers is, therefore, as intrinsically self-critical as the practices of those groups. Indeed, it is incorrect to say that "I watch" television. The viewer is always a "we" and the process of viewing always a social process.

3. The concentration of control over the mass media, the vehicles, has been on occasion inconsistent with the need to control informa-

tion; and in any case the private ownership of mass communication devices, the fact that such ownership denies social needs in favor of socially arbitrary and perpetually shifting alignments of people as audiences, is inevitably met with resistance. While this resistance is normally inchoate—that is, involving the subtle and artful transformation of each moment of the communication of messages to a moment of sociality and social awareness (cf. Sacks 1974; Garfinkel 1967)—it has its rationalized aspects as well. No history of communications could be complete without reference to the existence of constantly insistent alternatives poised in one form or another against official communiques (cf. Jones 1971; Thompson 1975; Neuberg 1977; Bakhtin 1968)—broadsides, songs, bills, anonymous letters, underground news-sheets, pirate radio, handouts and posters, street speeches, study groups, and so on.

Each of these changes in communicative disposition shows the vulnerability of even the most advanced technologies of capitalist control to the contradictions of private ownership with the needs and interest of society. The new media, with their reliance on phasing and sequence, socialized consumption, and highly concentrated class control, inevitably evoke these contradictions and engage their corresponding practices.

In the first case, opposition is built into the response—the fit of electronically generated material to the processes of ordinary discourse limits the power of "the medium" to be "the message," or form to dominate content within the message. In the second case, the socialization of consumption, like that of labor, introduces the perspectives and enforces the practices of collectivities. The result is again the insinuation of a critical context in precisely those situations designed to eliminate the prospect of criticism. In the third case, opposition arises from the visibility of capital's removal of a socially necessary resource, its attempted expropriation of the social media, and from the fact that any genuinely popular culture—diverse, interactive, and internally tolerant—will generate vehicles that preserve its authenticity in these respects.[4]

Ideology and Propaganda

Marxian research on the establishment of ideological frames and the dissemination of specific types of propaganda has tended to focus on "institutions" such as educational organizations and the licensed media (cf. Bowles and Gintis 1976; Schiller, 1971; Gitlin 1980; cf. various issues of the journal *Media, Culture, and Society,* especially vol. 6, no. 1, January, 1984, and no. 3, July, 1984). Recent American studies have drawn on European methodological traditions in order to recover content from its impoverished place in "content analysis" without, at the same time, reifying it. These traditions have also cultivated a more subtle sense of mediations than is available in the American social psychological emphases on "context," "setting," and "interpersonal influence" (cf. Williams 1977; Barthes 1972; Kristeva 1968; Foucault 1973; Althusser 1971; Ricoeur 1976; Jameson 1981; Eagleton 1983; and cf. issues of the journal *Social Text*).

Their main emphasis is discourse conceived as something other than language proper—something that defies structuration, is nonreiterative in its process, establishes meaning in regard to both the local situation of linguistic use and its context, and represents a form of subjectivity that does not reduce itself to individual psychology. In all these respects, Bakhtin's work is fundamental for its location of discourse within the dialectic of the *popular* with its heterogeneity and equality of voices, and the *official,* with its insistence on orders of stratification among voices (cf. Bakhtin 1968; 1981). The influence of the European studies has also begun to legitimize certain American studies, particularly ethnomethodology, that had been largely purged from social science during the 1970s (cf. Heritage 1984).

Among the newly prominent topics are the origin of messages, their structural properties, meaning, and significance within concrete discursive and interactive situations, types of imagery that emerge at the crest of proliferating ideological material, the character of social life that allows what is presented as message inevitably to be reconstituted as a volatile element of more general and nonreiterative discourses, and the asemantic and nonsemiotic features of conversation that reproduce the pragmatic conditions of conversational discourse (cf. Garfinkel 1967 for a classical statement).

The "origin" of messages refers not merely to their point of embarcation, but to the principle of authority that warrants them or to the competence that they display in content or form. The question of what a message consists of is part of this research, since "content" can mean what terms refer to, how they relate to each other, or the type of sociality they constitute—their sense. Questions that can be raised in these regards are: for whom or what does the message speak? what is the content for which this authority needs to be established? what is the context that makes the authority of the message both compelling and problematic? what becomes of a message once it is disseminated and received?

The critique of capital raises these questions in the context of the contradiction of economy with society, the developed expression of class analysis; and its method, as critique, provides a framework within which they can be discussed. Three aspects have been particularly prominent in the critical literature: the "structure," or internal ordering, of messages; the processes involved in their dissemination and cognition; and the dynamic aspects and role of contexts in determining the relation of abstracted structure and process.

The "structure of a message" is its capacity to render a subject matter definite and apparently complete, and/or its capacity to secure the relationship between two aspects of content—sense and authority. The abstraction of structure, the interiority of the message or correlation of content with boundary, allows theory to identify a message with a subject matter, a sense of the significance of that subject matter, and the authority constituted by the message independent of its critical aspects (cf. chap. 2, above).

Analysis of "a message" in terms of its structural aspects establishes it as a product of a more general intention: it shows an arrangement of the set of materials taken to be a message in such a way that the "recipient" of that precise message would not be one to take exception to it, that any further development of meaning is foreclosed, that the message has the capacity to fix consciousness. The ideological intention aims at producing structure as reality rather than as an aspect that is shown in the course of a critical analysis. To the extent to which this aim can be realized, the recipient is shown in a position of relative passivity, uninterested in the critical dimension of "communicative exchange" (cf. Garfinkel 1967; Brown 1983–4; Blum and McHugh 1984).

"Content" means for this research the fundamental terms and discursive conventions that provide the background of any credible message, features that must be at least implicit if the message is to be seen as part of the sense people make together. Context is then a matter of practice and occasion and is, to some extent, beyond the control of particular media or authority (cf. above). It provides, among other things, a referential base that allows the objects of ideological communication to be familiar and convenient to ordinary uses of language, and to participate in the fluency of the discourses in which their reception is imbedded. An adequate referent is not simply one that can occur regularly and with reliable recognizability, it must have some determinate location within the "lexical field" and discursive conventions that are its background, as well as some historical connection with the collectivities within which individuals find themselves as subjects (Garfinkel refers to such subjects as "members to settings" [1967]).

"Imagery," as emergent in discourse, is an epiphenomenon of communication, a kind of figured mood in regard to presented objects that depends heavily upon context. It is difficult to manage, and therefore is produced primarily through techniques of proliferation. To succeed as imagery, signs must be generated with minimal space between them (cf. Sacks 1974), so that each moment is followed swiftly by the next before the critical capacity is engaged. Emergent imagery is then the product of an over-accumulation of signs no one of which is ever fully available for scrutiny and review (Brown, 1983/4).[5]

The ambiguity of social life in capitalist society is apparent in the perpetual and unrelieved confusions between what is serious and what is casual, the rational and the nonrational, official requirements and the imperatives of civility, power and morality, "private troubles" and "public issues," control and autonomy, and obligation and experience. On the one hand this allows for easy reinforcement of ideology and imposes a sense of the moral necessity of official sanction even within areas of ostensible freedom—if confusion is to be relieved. On the other hand, it burdens everything that is "communicated" and "received" with contradiction and thus gives its content a definite historical dynamism regardless of intention (Goffman 1961b).

The methods involved in researching these and other topics are complex and their applications intricate (cf. Barthes 1972 for an early statement from the point of view of semiology; cf. Sacks 1974 and Garfinkel 1967 for a different, more sociological, point of view). While they comprise a separate study from Marxian political economy, their validity as methods for the critique of ideology depends upon what that theory brings to light.

The fact that the "production of ideology" inevitably engages opposition does not mean that the spheres of public discourse or even the academic disciplines that are dependent upon those spheres are characterized by free dialogue, any more than that the production of commodities by contradictory operations implies a genuine freedom of contract. American history is replete with examples of the suppression of ideas, political intentions, and organizations. Indeed, the attempt to suppress radical criticism of capitalism has been the rule rather than the exception (cf. Wolfe 1973; Rogin 1967; Gross 1980; Brown and Goldin 1973). Typically, radical dissent has been tolerated only when it has lacked political power, its proponents have lacked reputation, and its organizational expressions have been weak. At that limit one finds the active suppression of opposition by informal restrictions of political activism and expression, formal censorship of the media and official harassment of dissenters, and, too often, the use of the full measure of coercion available to capital and its state. All of these and more were in evidence during the 1960s and 1970s, as they have been throughout American and Western history (Miliband et al. 1984).

Despite the fact that opposition has occasionally found its issues and its voice beyond the inchoate texture of resistance that is implicit in capitalist production, the overall result remains: a public sphere dominated, problematically to be sure, by official ideologies compatible with or favoring the interests of capital against those of labor, and private property against society, whatever the propaganda used to convey these ideologies and whatever the methods used to suppress dissent.

Culture

Thus far, we have taken the possibility of speaking of "capitalist culture" for granted. It is fair to say that the contemporary Marxian literature on culture is as extensive and has achieved the same stature as its critique of capital (cf. Aronowitz 1981). The result has been a rich documentation of the cultural presence of the capitalist mode of production, the beginnings of an historical analysis, a dialectic of that presence, and considerable research on the relationship between culture, politics, and "class consciousness" (cf. Thompson 1963; Samuel 1981; Williams 1977; Eagleton 1983).

The documentation of capitalist culture has focused more often than not on consumerism (cf. Lefebvre 1971; Schneider 1975; Ewen 1976). We have already discussed the virtual prevalence of the commodity form, the corresponding fetishism of things, and the consequent loss of moral ground that characterize capitalism. Consumerism—beyond its surface of hyperactive buying—is the practical but uncritical realization of the ideological themes of the universal market: private property (the market in "collectibles"), individual initiative ("comparison shopping"), risk ("investment"), decision ("smart shopping"), exchange, and the denigration of work in favor of an ethic of purchasing nonconsumables. Under these auspices, human interaction consists in part of exercises in evaluating, bargaining, calculating, suspecting, evading, accounting, and the constant divestment of value.

Henri Lefebvre has gone beyond documentation to the expression "bureaucratic society of controlled consumption" to describe the social order that supports these practices (1971); but if the hallmarks of capitalism are uneven development, contradiction, and volatility, totalizing forms such as bureaucracy can never be fully achieved without undermining capitalism itself. Lefebvre's expression suggests that modern capitalism has moved beyond itself into the initial stages of fascism or corporatism (cf. Gross 1980).

Clearly, fascism has been one of capital's solutions in this century to the crisis aspects of the contradiction of classes. In this respect, U.S. policy in Latin America resembles German policy in Europe in the 1930s and 1940s. Whether it or something like it can be realized in the United States domestically is a much discussed issue (cf. Gross 1980). But it does not follow that because "big business" attempts to extend its global sway through the development or reinforcement of fascism (the state-sponsored class-based discipline of the work force) abroad that its home countries are fascist. While there is every reason to fear the mixture of right-wing politics, corporate control of government, ethnocentric violence, and the emergence of a new over-consuming and anti-societal entrepreneurial class fraction, and while the fascist tendency has become alarmingly visible in American politics in the wake of the Reagan ascendance, it is important to maintain the perspective implicit in the critique of capital: the contradictions of capitalist development are every bit as evident as the progress of capital itself, and through those it is possible to witness and envision new forms of opposition, already apparent in Europe, the United States, and the Third World (cf. Piven and Cloward 1982; Aronowitz 1983; Jameson 1984; Laclau and Mouffe 1985).[6]

Perhaps Lefebvre's failure adequately to acknowledge the concrete oppositional tendencies inherent in even the most extensive variants of capitalist control led him to see a greater practical totalization of the capitalist interest than is historically possible; or it may be that the shock of the European experience of fascism and the postwar global reconstitution of corporate capital in Europe encouraged the bias. Certainly, the emergence of Thatcher and Reagan has contributed to the growing sense of despair one sees today among proponents of socialist democracy. If, however, we consider his work as a structural analysis in the sense described above, we can see in it an attempt to model the intention of capital against the alternative intention of the society of the producers. But the capitalist intention/interest totally to dominate society is not new, though the society it intends to subsume is quite different from the national societies of the nineteenth century and though the weapons—fiscal and military—at its command seem of a different order of competence from any time in the past. The fact that there seems to be a new twist to this dynamism of capital provides at least some of the impetus behind the rereading of Lefebvre as well as current attempts to rethink the strategies of the left (cf. issues of *Monthly Review* since 1980; Hobsbawm 1981; Gorz 1976; Aronowitz 1981; Davis 1980a; Laclau and Mouffe 1985).

Thus, it is still instructive to hear Lefebvre refer to the market-based society as one of interpersonal "terror," because evaluating, bargaining, calculating, and the rest can only occur to the extent to which sociality is suppressed in principle, history denied, and evidence of exploitation made inadmissible (cf. Goffman 1963 and Habermas 1973). To be treated as lacking history is to be seen as incapable of surprise, lacking dynamism and creativity, something less than human. The practice of treating another as lacking history involves as well a self-protective attitude of eternal surveillance and a corresponding vigilance against the possibility of one's also being "found out." When generalized, this invokes a recognition of one's self as subject to precisely such treatment, as Goffman has so brilliantly dramatized in his book *Stigma* (1963). The obligations of this are clear: to evade being the object of possibly denigrating scrutiny but to carry out that constabulary function on others—to scapegoat. Under such circumstances, there is little room for the sense of tragedy so essential to an ethics of ends rather than means, an ethics of responsibility rather than expediency, an ethics in which humanity is the highest value. To the extent to which these obligations have become part of our socialization, we find it difficult to speak and therefore to think in terms of contradiction, dialectic, and history, and difficult to tolerate the reading and serious study of those traditions that make these issues vital (cf. Horkheimer and Adorno 1972; Habermas 1970c; Schroyer 1973).

This particular reflection led some neo-Marxians in the 1940s— refugees from Nazi Germany—to participate in the writing of one of the most prominent books in American social psychology, *The Authoritarian Personality* (Adorno et al. 1950). The book provided a theory of the type of personality prone to support right-wing ideas and practices. The roots of that type lay in a pathology of need. Because of the unpredictability and punitiveness of parental authority, the subjection of the child to a terrorist family regime at the early stages of life, the authoritarian individual lacks an internal set of personal controls and therefore a genuine moral sensibility. In the process of this separation of the individual from the social source of evaluative criteria, the child must learn to anticipate the will of authority and therefore to ignore that of peers. Because the key to the success of this domestic regime is the fear the child comes to have of all authority, he or she must also learn to suppress from consciousness the ambivalent feelings occasioned by that fear and the possibility that recognizing that authority might under certain conditions have rational grounds (be subject to choice). To admit those feelings and that recognition would be to admit as well the hatred that is part of so extreme an experience, and therefore to subject one's self to anxiety over possible reprisal. The loss of empathy for others and insight into oneself creates a certain general blindness to life, a stubborn rejection of its joys, sufferings, and weaknesses in favor of abstract and thus only enforceable principles (cf. also below). Evidences of those then appear as indices of chaos and subversion. The extension of this into racist ideology, political intolerance, patriotism, violence, support for militarism, fundamentalisms of all sorts, love of heroes, and a need to exercise total control over desire and expressivity are said to be part of the mixture of extreme defensiveness and equally extreme aggressivity that is the most evident characteristic of the authoritarian type. It is clear that such a personality would be unable to tolerate even a glimmer of the dynamism of history and to bear the personal and social revelations that must accompany an awareness of that dynamism.

To the extent that the model describes a possibility, one can argue that the universal market is made to order for the expressive qualities and practices available to the type. But it does not follow that fascism is the result of the generation of the authoritarian syndrome through the agency of a specific type of family configuration, or that authoritarianism has its own distinct history (as is suggested by Milgram [1974], and by the authors themselves, based on a rather mechanistic reading of psychoanalysis). If fascism is the result of an epidemic of authoritarianism, how can the latter's conditions be explained? It is sufficient, at this stage in the development of our discussion, to note that it is already possible to show in the critique of capital the antisocietal "totalitarian" potential of capitalism and its support for at least the practices if not the consciousness of authoritarianism.

The Authoritarian Personality poses the issue of the intersection of personal and social history. But it remains an essentially dispositionalist theory of character: strict and arbitrarily punitive child-rearing fixes in the character a permanent need to seek control for the self when internal self-control is impossible. The social form in which this need is realized depends on the expressive opportunities available in society, with a severely stratified social order likely to provide the manifestations of character associated with fascism. What is missing is an analysis of the ways in which a capitalist order of everyday life— with its rigorous division of thought, work, and pleasure—socializes character at each moment of its operation and throughout the lives of its individuals. Despite its disclosures about the nature of integrated conservative thought—the irrepressibility of the links among patriotism, ethnocentrism, intolerance, lack of insight, projectivity, and fear of difference—and its obvious value for the study of the fascist potential, *The Authoritarian Personality* remains dependent upon an unarticulated sociology that links subjectivity with the scale of modern capitalism and the historical dynamic of its mode of production. Given that, even so apparently rigid and determined a character type as "the potential fascist" would have to be reformulated in terms of its own contradictions, and the principle of authority reconceptualized in terms of its positive, historically valid, as well as its negative attributes.

Whether or not consumerism and fascism are historical aspects of the expansiveness of capital or just variations of its more general incompatibility with sociality, they illustrate the relationship between the critique of ideology and the more general critique of culture. They also illustrate how too great an emphasis on specific practices or attitudes taken in abstraction from their more complex and dynamic contexts can lead away from historical critique toward a cultural perspective that too easily loses its connection with history. This is one of the areas of controversy in the contemporary Marxian literature in which theory is undergoing elaboration and reconstruction (cf. Thompson 1978; Anderson, 1980; cf. the journal *Social Text)*. Gramsci's writings have been important for the complications of Marxism they offer to this controversy (cf. Laclau and Mouffe 1985), but they have been used more for their suggestion that culture is a relatively autonomous structure than for their historical and dialectical materialism. As a result, Gramsci has been placed in a theoretical context that leads some writers toward an abstracted structural-functionalism in which the cultural factor supercedes the economic. In that case, the study of culture produces its own theory and method independent of the historical materialism and dialectical reason that made the Gramscian insight possible in the first place.

Perhaps the most promising epistemologically grounded discussions of cultural tendencies and processes consistent with Marxism derive from philosophy and literary theory (cf. Eagleton 1983; Williams 1977) and, less explicitly, from the work of two American sociologists trained primarily in the non-Marxian critical traditions of their discipline, Erving Goffman and Harold Garfinkel. Goffman's is the most sustained sociologically critical examination of the cultural practices of Americans currently available, though it lacks explicit theoretical clarification and is posed in terms that are apparently ahistorical. Garfinkel's is the most methodologically and epistemologically sophisticated attempt to reformulate all of sociology as the microhistorical analysis of conversational discourse and to gauge its significance for the identification of the principle of subjectivity in social theory.

Both scholars are remarkable for the rigor with which they pursue their insights and for the singular accessibility of their work to other disciplines. Neither is fully intelligible outside of the inclusive framework of dialectical reason and its historical critique of capital. Their research is indispensable for any serious discussion of "class consciousness" that refers both to its contradictions and practical realizations. A brief account of one part of Goffman's work illustrates its potential for a Marxian theory of culture and its compatibility with the neo-Marxian emphasis on consumerism that has been as suggestive as it has been problematic. Following that, in chapter 10, Garfinkel's work will be discussed in the context of a more general examination of the concept of "class consciousness."

Goffman's writing intersects the major non-Marxian critical disciplines in American social science—psychoanalysis, discourse analysis, phenomenology, ethnomethodology, and symbolic interactionism—

and brings to light certain critical implications of the functionalist tradition as represented by Talcott Parsons. The relevance of Goffman's research to Marxian analysis lies in its investigation of interactions among people who take for granted that their activities will be treated as performances (instances of an abstraction of activity) and judged by "objective" standards of structural or functional appropriateness. The keynote is the impulse to incessant comparison without reference to value, in other words universal exchange as a principle of interpersonal interaction (1963).

Goffman has taken as the object of his research precisely the type of subjectivity for which capitalist production and its market are the full extent of objective reality. Like Lefebvre, he has idealized, or abstracted, his pehnomenon in order to draw attention to it as a practical tendency of the society virtually constituted by capital (cf. Goffman, 1963, 1961b, 1959), though nowhere is there an explicit reference to capitalism in his work. What critics have found particularly troublesome in Goffman is his overemphasis on calculation and manipulation, the politics of everyday life. If, however, we consider this a critical abstraction intended to highlight the tendencies of its context, the overemphasis is acceptable on condition that the context can be made explicit. The following interpretation attempts to show that the societal context that makes his discussion of the politics of everyday life intelligible is precisely that described in the Marxian critique of capital.

Goffman foregrounds the mutual surveillance and vigilance of people awaiting judgment at every turn. People enter social settings uneasily, aware that anything they do can be labelled and as such might be made socially significant and subject to interpretation based on information over which they have no clear control. Under certain circumstances, what they do can be the basis for the assignment of a "social identity" that bears on their acceptability as members. At the limit of social interaction, then, all members anticipate the possibility of being rejected by their fellows as the result of a collective determination. As a result, their orientations to social life are tactical, their manipulations desperate: they must conceal what they can or be seen as bearing what may be a "shameful defect," or "stigma," that would if disclosed be grounds for their rejection. Or, where the defect has already been disclosed they must find some way of diminishing the tension their presence as "deviant" creates for the interacting group.

In fact, every gesture, every word spoken, might be seen as indicating an inappropriate, unacceptable, "virtual social identity," an identity attributed to the individual on the basis of a collectively realized interpretation. Thus, interactants are never relieved of the problems of *controlling information* so that what they must conceal remains concealed, and *managing tension* so that what they nevertheless have already revealed does not cause the sociality of the group to deteriorate (cf. 1961b; 1961a; 1963).

The assignment of traits on the basis of visible behavior is part of the social enforcement of an indefinite process of invidious comparison. That assignment is inevitable because of the facts that: 1. people are always conveying information that they neither intend to nor can control, particularly through nonverbal means of communication; 2. the fragility with which group boundaries are established and maintained requires the constant discovery of unacceptable identities in order to test and reconfirm those boundaries; 3. the invasion of every local situation by an intrusive context increases the likelihood that people will encounter each other more as occasions for mutual evaluation than as partners in an exchange or a piece of work; 4. in order to avoid the peril of rejection one must avoid its possibility, and this requires constant effort to assign socially denigrating status characteristics to others, making everyone liable to rejection because of what they are seen to be rather than what they do.

To the extent to which this constitutes the culture of a given setting, the one constant will be the attempt by parties to disguise themselves in such a way that the disguise takes on the appearance—even to the one disguised—of an authentic self, an "actual social identity." The most obvious tactic for this involves distraction and the most easily managed distractions involve scapegoating: every group generates a distinct category of "the abnormal" no matter how expressed, to which all parties are potentially liable and which all parties constantly subject to political manipulation. Goffman generalizes the point in order to argue that the standard category of the abnormal is a political construct and that its culture, the culture of the distinction, is essentially defensive: we are not normal in the abstract or absolutely "objective" sense but only in the dialectical sense of being "normal against" others.

It should be obvious that the socially constitutive problematic of acceptance/rejection, so marvelously identified by Goffman, cannot be held to be a general problem of human nature. It is necessary—and Goffman begs the question but does not preclude it—to inquire into the historically dynamic context in which the sort of alienation he describes is intelligible to theory. One finds a hint of this more elaborate inquiry into "context" in the work of some of Goffman's students (cf. Sudnow 1967). The outlines of such an inquiry are suggested in our discussions of labor and labor power, and in the individual or local ramifications of the socialization of production. The concept of "replaceability," grounded in the critique of capital, serves as an adequate point of departure. It suggests the types of conditions necessary for the interactions Goffman describes: for the codification of conduct as traits and the assignment of social identities on the basis of which people can be accepted or rejected; for the obligation to dissemble that all parties must recognize in order to participate in the practice of classification and deal with their own vulnerability to that practice; for the depersonalization necessary if those deemed unworthy are to be practically excluded without leaving unmanageable traces of affect; and for the managerial detachment in the representation of self that must be embodied in such interactions and that marks them as analogous to the class relation of property to labor power, economy to society. Goffman gives a more detailed and suggestive rendering of the "terrorism" implicit in interpersonal relations in capitalism than does Lefebvre; but he lacks what Lefebvre insists is necessary, an analysis of the historical possibility of what he describes.

In any case, Goffman's work is suggestive for a Marxian theory of culture in which what is at stake is not a structure of thought or affect but a process of realizing the contradictory and therefore unrealizable commodity form of the individual. In this, it presupposes the incorporation of people into the historical processes of capitalist development and, in so doing, suggests a practical infraprocess for what has been called "class consciousness."

Notes

1. Perhaps the most startling representation of this dichotomy is found in the film *Rambo*, a vengeance movie in which a Vietnam veteran returns to free U.S. prisoners enslaved as farm hands by sadistic Vietnamese under the control of Russians. Rambo dispatches hundreds of the Asiatic horde and returns to threaten the bureaucrats who made the war unwinnable in the first place and who continue to deny recognition to the Americans who fought in Indochina. It is impossible to see the film without thinking of Nazi propaganda—the falseness of its representations is only one aspect; its sensual play of pain and revenge, its stereotypes, its elevation of the violent, inarticulate, race/nation patriotic hero, and its contempt for what is civil in society, are key, as is its impatience with deliberation, compromise, and the values of humanism. Man against machine, race against race, national spirit against its own national government, woman as victim and supplicant, strength as the test of goodness are all subthemes to this curiosity of our times. What is important about it in regard to the dichotomization of society and its other is the proliferation of icons and references connected with the film, and its sheer popularity. It is as if *Rambo* expresses a great relief, as if it attempts to, and succeeds at least to some extent, purge the United States of the guilt and self-criticism and recognition of the complexity of the world that the invasion of Indochina produced. That members of Congress watched the film just before passing legislation

favoring an even more bellicose response to "communism" than before, that the president has referred to the film in describing his own foreign policy aspirations, and that the weapons depicted in the film have become iconic to so many survivalist-oriented Americans, make its appearance at this time even more disquieting. That it flaunts its own falsehoods in the effort to create the form of righteous revenge gives it a biblical quality and intellectual indifference that fits the "fundamentalism" that is currently so vital a part of the American crisis.

2. That a book is reread in some sense does not imply either that it is a "text" or that a second move through its pages produces the same result as the first (cf. Barthes 1977). The form that resists reference to context consists of the contradiction of physical distinctness (consumability) and the structures that are apparent through several readings and that dispose the reader to know it as an instance of language rather than speech (its circulatability). A book, in other words, cannot be lost.

3. Cf. Bakhtin, 1968, for a discussion of this "carnivalized" use of language that he argues persuasively for as a constitutive feature of what we call "society."

4. Cf. Habermas's attempt to identify a moment of sociality in any process of communication (1970b). At a different level of analysis, Raymond Williams has attempted to identify the critical relationship between the various and competing hegemonic cultures of capitalism (1977). Jameson has attempted to establish the relationship between vehicles of communication and the subjective aspect of history, further complicating the discussion of hegemony (1981). Cf. Bakhtin's remarkable discussion of the characteristics of popular culture and the limitations they impose on official culture (1968), and Brown's related discussion of the paradoxical relationship between the textualizing media and nonreiterative processes of establishing culture (1983). Thompson's invocation of underlife in his accounts of counterhegemonic popular manifestations still remains the most important empirical analysis for contemporary theory (1963, 1975).

5. Television advertising has provided the most obvious examples—where the space between purchase and consumption is filled with proliferating furnishings of everyday life and the icons and monuments of officially enscribing culture: elements of work, play, domesticity, and intimacy, mixed with emblems of nation, wealth, and production.

6. Cohen and Rogers (1983) have provided a summary of the sort of documentation available for discussing the possibility of something like fascism, and Gross (1980) has put this sort of material in the context of an analysis of the "friendly fascism" he sees as a distinct trend in the United States. Chomsky and Herman have documented the fascist element of U.S. foreign policy as well as anyone (1979).

10

Class Consciousness

DESPITE THE PROSPECTS for establishing a philosophically defensible link between theoretical concept and empirical interpretation, the study of class consciousness remains mired in their separation. There seem to be at least two general reasons: 1. Marxian theory can only be applied to the historical practices for which it is appropriate if it is formulated as dialectical reason—if it clarifies and displays the principles of contradiction, the irreversibility of history, the self-transforming relations of subjectivity and objectivity and theory and practice, and the mediations by which the historical principle is conserved in any abstraction or "empirical case."

Dialectical reason has not found favor in American philosophy and social science, perhaps in part for reasons mentioned above. In any case, the exclusion of the dialectical tradition from the academy was, until very recently, virtually complete in sociology, political science, philosophy, and psychology. It is only in the last decade that advances in literary studies have so influenced the philosophy of language, conceptions of mediation, and historiography that there seems no choice for the social sciences but to come to terms with the forgotten dialectical criticism on which those disciplines originally depended. Nevertheless, the temptation remains to use these studies heuristically, as sources of insight rather than to face their radical implications for sociology and social theory. In that case, they provide at best challenges to the validity of conventional descriptive categories. At worst, their use in the mode of abstracted empiricism undermines theory altogether by shifting the burden of disciplines to the further calculation of reality and away from the task of gauging the significance of events within a socially viable conception of history. In fact, most of what passes for Marxian research in the social sciences, no matter that it has had enormous critical value, still refers back to quantitative empirical methodologies (cf. Wright 1978; Flacks and Turkel 1978; Burawoy 1979a). These methodologies are, however, consistent with the epistemological requirements of Marxian theory only when their results are not taken to be knowledge of last resort and the scope of their employment is restricted to its proper discursively critical context.

2. Where methods consistent with those requirements have been developed, whether specifically articulated with the critique of capital or not, they have been treated as exotic, assigned the status of "micro" analysis, or simply purged from the academy. To some extent this has been the case with ethnomethodology and the related discipline that Alan Blum and Peter McHugh call "analysis" (1984). Ethnomethodologists have for the most part, been allowed to teach only when their work is seen as identifying a topic otherwise neglected (as in "conversational analysis"), complementing standard disciplines without disturbing paradigmatic claims, representing an application of standard methodology, or expressing an acceptable "classical" tradition—exemplified by Weber, Durkheim, Schutz, or Parsons, among others.

Marxians have as often criticized these new methodologies as non-Marxians, perhaps testimony to the institutional accommodation that is necessary for the theory itself to be taught or to the fact that Marxian academicians are, after all, academicians subject to the particular mediations that qualify education and educational work in a capitalist society. While it is possible to argue for the competence of the criticisms independent of these reasons, it remains the case that they often reflect minimal reading of the relevant literature, give too short shrift to the ideas that one would normally expect of the genuinely critical temper, or rely on oversimplified versions of the new disciplines (cf. Piccone 1975-76, for an early theoretically interesting neoMarxian critique of ethnomethodology that nevertheless suffers from these defects).

The major topics of that research on "class consciousness" that have been linked successfully with Marxian theory are discussed by Raymond Williams (1977) as elaborations or qualifications of the concept of "hegemony." Williams points out that a culture of domination always engages a counterculture of resistance, that neither is homogeneous but each aims at an "hegemony"—a universalization in practice that is impossible in principle, and that "class consciousness" must be seen as an instance of resistance at the level of class-mediated institutions rather than as behavior, something in people's minds, or expressions of discrete and measurable attitudes and opinions (cf. also Adorno 1976).

The following studies fall within this program: 1. the practices of social formations (governments, parties, unions, and so on) by which individuals and groups are situated within the contradictions of capitalist production (cf. Poulantzas 1975a, 1975b); 2. the underlying texture of resistance that corresponds to those contradictions and that constitues a permanent mobilization of labor as a virtual society of producers (cf. Thompson 1963); 3. the orders of organization, power, ideology, and event that constitute what sociologists call "collective behavior" and that account for the movement of labor beyond a merely economistic resistance (cf. Wolfe 1973; Brown and Goldin 1973; Rudé 1964); 4. the political and discursive practices that give focus to mobilizations and manifest an historically significant integration of class interest (cf. Blackburn 1978; Eagleton 1983; cf. Lukacs 1971); 5. the self-critical element within a mobile class of producers understood and illustrated in ways intended to show the development of that class as a society, in terms of its capacity to "learn" and to "have" history (cf. Sartre 1976; Clastres 1977).

"Class consciousness" has become so distinct and developed an area of study that interest in it now extends beyond political sociology to culture and history. It has come to cover the field of human activity considered in its critical aspect, including at least some connection to the earlier studies of the labor movement and the revolutions on which its integrity as a topic originally depended (cf. Ollman 1971; Gabel 1975).

The literature on "class consciousness" grew to maturity after World War II, when a number of writers influenced by the Marxian tradition, became impatient with the pace of development and the political prospects of the European and American working classes (cf. Anderson 1976). Part of this impatience was no doubt due to an evaluation of labor's prospects in regard to the political movements and associations that were its contemporary expressions, as if labor had no history but that of its momentary accomplishments (cf., for example, Wellmer 1971). Another part was due to a reaction to the Stalin experience, certainly understandable as a matter of principle but also partly a reflection of earlier and continuing disputes among organizations and organizational fragments on the left (cf. Hobsbawm, 1973).

The bitterness of those disputes and the intensity of their intellectual justifications may account for the current tendency to see in Stalinism evidence of an incurable disposition to totalitarianism extending in the most extreme cases from Marx through all contemporary versions of socialism, communism, and social movements that claim those names. What had been a close and often profound analysis of the Soviet experience became instead a foundation for a certain anti-leftism within the left, centering on Marxian theory and hostile to social movements that display any trace whatsoever of what Gramsci called the "moment" of "bureaucratic centralism"—as if the latter were an organizational trait (growing inevitably from the conflict implications of theory) within the more general critical category of "domination" rather than a "moment" of an historical conjuncture that must be both self-critically tolerated and as self-critically transformed. One result, an inability to take sides, has introduced an unfamiliar note of cynicism on the left that currently threatens its historically critical tradition.

On the other hand, the elevation of "critical theory" to a position beyond history encouraged the critique of everyday life which in turn was elaborated as a new critique of culture in which "consciousness" figured as a psychological distortion determined by a "systematic" distortion of communication (cf. Habermas 1971, 1975; Wellmer 1971; Schroyer 1973; Arato and Gebhardt 1978). The standard this literature intended to implement was that of total liberation taken in a curiously nonhistorical yet dialectical (and therefore idealistic) relation to total domination. But its significance was methodological and intellectual beyond the limitations of that project, as can be seen by the influence the journal *Telos* has had on American writing in the humanities and the social sciences. There was also an institutional effect that consisted of a partial détente between mainstream and radical sociology. The "critical" turn made an important connection between the tradition of Marx by way of Hegel and that of Max Weber, an authentic sociological "classic," and so contributed to the legitimacy of that turn and, ironically, of Marxian theory itself within the university. The emphasis on "subjectivity," "consciousness," and "reflexivity" seemed as well to provide a new "paradigm" for American sociologists, or at least a new problematic, that could satisfy their hunger for more than a recapitulation of 1950s ideology in the form of social theory (cf. Gouldner 1970).

Thus, what seemed even on the left to threaten the prospects of a renewed interest in Marx was partly responsible for that very interest, though one modified by the traditions of what Perry Anderson called, with some disdain for the emphasis on subjectivity that was its hallmark, "Western Marxism" (1976). Because of this emphasis, the reemergence of academic Marxism at the end of the 1970s was able to bring together the problematics of culture and consciousness in a way that seemed to challenge Marx's labor theory of value. The Marxian terminology was used in this context largely as categories for organizing ethnographic and historical information to indicate "formations" of consciousness. Significantly, the term "class" in "class consciousness" no longer referred to an historical movement or a category of operation within capitalist production, part of its dialectic; and the term "consciousness" began to lose its sense of a dialectical relation of subject and object (cf. Sartre, 1976).

One result of this challenge has been a divergence of interest between those casting about for new theories of socialism and those attempting to reinterpret Marxian theory or make it sufficiently elaborate to deal with the issues raised by its left critics. In any case, "class

consciousness" continues to influence the Marxian imagination, especially as part of the critique of ideology. It is necessary, therefore, to
discuss the possiblity of a formulation that is consistent with the
Marxian analysis of the capitalist mode of production.

The very use of the term "consciousness" seems to reduce what is
intended to be explained as a social phenomenon to percepts and ideas,
thereby suggesting a need for a general psychology of individuals at
least relatively independent of historical context. From this point of
view, "consciousness" typically refers either to the prevalence of
political awareness among the members of a class (taken as an empirical category) or to an individual person's awareness that he or she is a
member of a class and therefore shares a certain predicament with
others similarly situated in the relations of the social economy.

The first option has directed attention to public opinion, the spread
of propaganda, the general influences of the mass media, and the
"informal" or "improvised" processes that lie in the background of
rumor, crowd formation, and the development of social movements
(cf. Brown and Goldin 1973). It has raised what is for Marxian theory
an unanswerable, or unaskable, question: how is a population of
individuals recomposed as a social class? The question is not legitimate
for Marxian theory as such because the Marxian concept of class is not
an empirical category, a name for collections of people, or a term for
classifying individuals according to abstract criteria. It refers to an
operative principle of the capitalist mode of production, and therefore
to a relation of operative principles. Clearly someone must work and
someone must coordinate, someone must be employed as labor power
and someone must exploit that power if there is to be capitalist
production and a capitalist accumulation of wealth. The empirically
variable connection of class with distinct demographic groupings is
obvious. Operative principles must, after all, be operative. Despite the
temptation to ask it, the proper quesiton is not how people come to
think of themselves as members of a class, since until they have done
so the class cannot be said to exist (if "class" is defined by consciousness) and therefore capitalism would have been inconceivable in the
first place (and the problem of class consciousness would not have
arisen). It is, rather, how the class exploitative character of production
validates itself as a practical matter in the agglomerated, political, and
everyday affairs of the society of the producers.

Studies of "public opinion" document momentary orientations and
object-related affections as if people were not involved in social
production. To the extent to which those orientations and affections
overwhelm discourse, they suppress collective reflection on the role of
class in production. But this is a long way from providing theoretically
valid information on the course of development of "class conscious-

ness." For that, research on agglomerative forms (organizations, groups, and so on), political activities, and everyday affairs is indispensable (cf. chapter nine).

The second option has led to social psychological hypotheses about a variety of topics related to the formations of subjectivity: the socialization of children, the role of language in thought and group process, and the relationship of learning and motivation to perception, thought, and conduct. In this case, "consciousness" is defined in a strictly psychological and individualistic way that begs the question of sociohistorical context. There is no reason at present to preclude the possibility of a science of the intersection of personal and social histories. But it has neither been devised not yet shown to be essential to an adequate sociology of capitalism (cf. Sartre 1964, for a remarkable example of what such a study might look like).

"Class consciousness" should not be confused theoretically with the particular awareness of specific individuals or with groups or populations identified at one time or another as "the workers" or "the capitalists," though it is possible to recognize a class aspect to politically relevant motives in the midst of particular conflicts involving organized groups. If follows that the phrase is both curious and problematic: an operative principle, an agency, cannot have consciousness in the sense of being psychologically aware and self-responsive. It cannot have a psychology or be psychological though it must, if it is to have the quality of agency, nevertheless have subjectivity.

What sense then can be made of the idea if it is to apply to an operative principle of production, specifically that of labor taken as the society of the producers? There are, as we have seen, two manifestations of labor in capitalism: the concrete, momentary, object-related work of specific individuals—the specific job-related tasks that are being performed, and the abstract, generalized, alienated labor power that is never performed but only borne by individuals, and never theirs to keep but only theirs to sell. While it is doubtless profitable to study the former—attitudes toward task and self that are properties of individuals at work—only the study of labor power is relevant to the sociology of capitalism since that is the uniquely active principle of the expansion of capital as a societally creative force. This is not to deny the relevance of personal experience in principle, but only to insist that the issue of subjectivity be coordinated theoretically with the class operations historically specific to the capitalist mode of production (cf. Anderson 1980).

We have already seen that the bearing and selling of labor power as one's only resource for survival can be examined in its subjective aspect. We have so far, however, focussed on the limitations this must place on the self-awareness of individuals. The theory of class consciousness requires a more precise phenomenology that can point to the principles of action that govern the bearing and selling of labor power as well as its perpetual subjection to the will of another. These are the elements of the type of subjectivity properly referred to as "class" consciousness; but they can only be clarified as such if they are conceptually implicit in an authentic society of the producers and therefore exemplify cooperation as an historic force. Whether the following is acceptable or not, any adequate solution will have to be consistent with those requirements. Above all, it will have to avoid a reduction of the problem to a psychology of individuals and an account of their specific and variable states of awareness (shared or unique), just as it will have to avoid identifying individuals as embodiments of the categories of political economy.

Initially, it is important to recognize that every contextualized principle of operation must display a "reflexive" aspect, a principle of learning or reproduction, if it is to be something that humans do, if it is to be conceived of as action, and if it is to be capable of being part of an historical dynamic, a unity of opposing interests. For example, the movement of a ball across a field from one point to another describes the game of football, but only as something that can be done equally as well by humans and machines. The movement can be indefinitely repeated, but only through the application of a guiding impulse independent of it.

The description is inadequate if football is to be considered a contest consisting of the actions of people, part of a season of contests, and something in one relation or another to similar actions among those who comprise other teams or a league. In that case, one can only speak of the motion of the body and ball in connection with reasons that refer to relations: carrying the ball, kicking and throwing, taking positions, anticipating, developing strategy, and employing tactics. As such, football is defined by what people do and can do when they must select their acts within the confines of a set of rules and a context of opposing interests. To say that someone kicks the ball is to say more than that the leg moves and then the ball moves; it is to say that someone has made a decision in the context of a game and attempts to implement a purpose sensible within the divided collectivity that is the game's subject. Kicking the ball cannot be understood as part of a game unless it is seen as an instance of agency, an act chosen to realize a purpose that might be modified by the experience of having performed it, and as an act that is essentially collective, problematic, and contextually appropriate (cf. Blum and McHugh 1984).

If the operative principle is labor power in the context of production, 1. its subjective aspect must be the *reflexivity* of class, the way in which its bearing and selling and its subjection to the will of another is displayed in those very acts,[1] and 2. that aspect must be visible in the particulars of its exclusive exercise—in that bearing, selling, and subjection. We have already seen that the reason for bearing and selling labor power is to be subject to the will of another (in order to be productive), and that the visibility of its exercise depends on an account of the contradictions of the capitalist mode of production.

At its most abstract level, "class consciousness" is the incorporation in action of the separation of and relation between purpose and activity: every act that can be shown to be part of capitalist production must display, as a necessary feature of its adequate analysis, the lack of subjective purpose in what is nevertheless purposive activity, and the lack of necessity for any concrete act—because it is no more than one among an indefinite number of means to what appears to be a definite end.

For example, one would expect to find in the exercise of bearing a portion of labor power evidence of reluctance to bear and sell it, an autonomous movement (apart from its subjection to external control) toward repetition and routinization as reflexive to its being subject to the will of another, and an unwillingness of its bearers and sellers to accept revisions of the uses to which their energy is put. The evidence must be in the actions themselves, not merely in the individuals. The reluctance might be reflected in the relative priority given to bearing and selling, between going to work or calling in sick; the movement toward repetition and routinization might appear as a polarization of what individuals are obliged to do on the job and the non-job-related attractions present in the job situation; resistance to the revision of performance might be seen in subtle forms of sabotage—excessive concentration, an unwieldy insistence on a precision of ordering within tasks, and confusion in the implementation of the economically compulsory broadening of task requirements.

If the connection with the act is to be made even more explicit, one should analyze wage labor in terms of the tension implicit in something concrete bearing something abstract, the gap between decision and execution, and the inertia implicit in activity governed by external purposes.

It should be clear from this discussion that the reflexivity of labor power—class consciousness as labor power's self-referring practical inconsistency with itself—includes reference to the exploitative feature of production and therefore to the relations between the classes. For class consciousness to be the incorporation in action of the separation of and relation between purpose and activity, it must also refer to the capitalist mode of production—its essential contradictory operative principles. It should also be clear that it is a feature of action and not of mind: it is the way people behave if they are to be parties to capitalist production, not the way they might or might not believe, think, or feel. Class consciousness is, then, a property of production and not something that grows or recedes according to the education, training, and influence exercised over individuals or to the adequacy or lack thereof of culture or ideas.

This is not to deny the significance of abstractive empiricism for the discursive aspect of theory, that aspect that is vocal, collective, and immediately practical. The question is not so much the legitimacy or illegitimacy of a certain type of research but precisely where it fits in theory or in what theory makes evident. Empirical research, organized by topic and conducted by any method whatsoever, may find its way into the critique of capital, but only if there has been a prior determination of what might make it significant.

For example, structural analyses of texts, events, or formations provide abstractions of false consciousness—activity for which the question "why not do something else?" does not arise—that highlight the historical dimension of class struggle merely by idealizing antihistorical and reiterative forms. On the other hand, as we have seen, structuralism can have no more privileged a position within Marxism than that: it is a subsidiary methodology, though an important one. Similarly, experimental manipulations of human behavior, survey research, and models and simulations, are ordinarily used to establish a reality that is not recognizable from the Marxian point of view—one in which human beings are made up of dispositions that are relatively fixed and unmistakably expressed in utterances, endorsements, and movements of the body; engaged in idealizations of one sort of interaction or another regardless of context and history; and in no essential relationship with those who observe them.

It does not follow, however, that the standard literature or its procedures need to be rejected. Any adequate intervention in a prevailing literature must, in one way or another, use its discourses and methods and acknowledge what is tempting about them. To that extent, empirical materials of that sort are meaningful, but only as part of an argument that must never be permitted to take what it refers to and the certainty of its reference for granted. Work like William Domhoff's (1967, 1970, 1980) documents the networks of power brokers that make up the official and unofficial state and its infra-order. But it cannot disclose the nature or operation of the state, or its connection with and limits of its infra-order without having established its historical significance. It is primarily useful in engaging non-Marxian arguments about the democratic nature of modern capitalism in their own terms.

There is yet another way in which abstracted empiricism is relevant to the Marxian project, namely in its clarification of the objects presupposed in strategy. The politics of class struggle provide conditions for the application of Marxism that illustrate the difference between theory and practice and the tragic aspect of politics that corresponds to that difference—the fact that the moments of action are limited by their own contexts means that no analysis is fully adequate to their problems and that no guarantee of success can be given in advance. The articulation of the theoretical and practical critiques of capital is never a matter of certainty, since to be such, theory would have to be beyond history, and practice would have to be the passive reflection of theory.

Yet, there is a basis for a less than full articulation of the two that corresponds to what we have called the dialectic of their relationship. Our guiding principle for the solution to this problem is, by now, a familiar one: whatever is universal about society is established by the universalizing or totalizing development of the capitalist interest. Whatever oppositional interest is capable of absorbing the differences among people in a general interest that includes them all can only be one that is historically possible. The only general interests that capitalism prepares are those of labor and capital, and only the former is authentically capable of universalization. It does not follow that labor's interest can at any given time establish a satisfactory social order that includes every possible group, because not every group that exists at any given time is fully mediated by the dynamics of capitalism. The relationship between labor struggles and peasant revolts illustrates the problem and the limits of a socialist movement: merely because capitalism establishes a need to consolidate a society that it cannot consolidate, and because labor is the historical interest that corresponds to that need, and because the contradictions of capital leave no choice but to move toward a socialist movement of some sort, it does not follow that the pursuit of socialism will be immediately satisfying to all people.

The dynamic of capitalism forever precludes a return to small-scale property, subsistence production, or individualistic pursuits carried out independently of others altogether. This is so not just for capital's impulse but for that of labor as well. That this is so does not mean that one says "a pox on both your houses," since that would be to take the position outside of history that ultimately endorses cynicism and passivity. The struggle for society cannot but take place, whether successfully or not; and because of the limitations posed by the very form that creates the need—capitalist production—that struggle will have its own internal differences the solutions of which cannot be decided in advance. And it will have differences with those who yet lie outside of capitalist economy to a sufficient degree that the universal interest it constitutes can only be theoretically universal for them, not practically so.

For example, an end to exploitation was a formal interest of European craftsmen in the nineteenth-century, but because the independent craftsman was not exploited in the same way that the worker was, that interest could not have become a socially practical one. The craftsman's income and, to some extent, conditions of work, were influenced by the growth of the capitalist mode of production. But craftsmen were not obliged to sell their capacity to work as labor power. It follows that a socialist movement is both necessary and inevitably incomplete, and that the relation of theory and practice cannot be fully articulate, yet practice can only include reference to the universal possibility of its interest if it is theoretical in the sense of being self reflective. It also follows that the politics of compromise are both unavoidable and pose problems for the further development of society that must be unsettling to those whose practice represents a universal interest. Finally, it follows that the use of theory in political circumstances involves something on the order of what we have called abstraction. As part of politics, it is governed more strictly by momentary or conjunctural considerations than historical, and it is reflexive to more than class. Political acts represent themselves in terms of needs, organizations, and conditions that appear independent of the contradictions of capitalism. Yet, their capacity to supercede the differences among needs, organizations, and conditions depends on the type of reflection—critical or not, historical or empiricist—that those politics allow beyond their immediate causes and occasions: because capitalism establishes the general conditions of its society, to the extent that there are general conditions, and through the workings of its contradictory mode of production establishes a relation of historical conditions to the only universal interest possible under capitalist economy—the end of exploitation in favor of the *society* of the producers.

Because of these limitations, theory in relation to politics tends to be object-oriented such that it, momentarily, takes for granted the historical critique and transforms it into a relatively fixed set of assumptions from which strategic reflection can take place. Labor struggles need the occasional survey, though only that done in regard to needs articulated in the course of struggle. Grass-roots politics needs to specify the terrain on which power operates, if only because it organizes through the communication of program and the cultivation of a sense that militancy will be both valid and reliable—suited to what is known and both collective and otherwise rational. Party-building requires both the capacity to intervene in prevailing discourses and literatures and codifications of interactions the enforcement of which, or reinforcement of which, can be acceptable by those to whom a party wishes to appeal. Note that here, as with any survey or experiment, the question is not what people will do, as if a study of what they do is sufficient to predict what they will do, but what room there is in what people do for a party or class organization to attract attention, engage interest, and mobilize sentiment and participation. The findings of empirical research are models of what might be done in approaching people, not facts, predictions, or laws.

This discussion of class consciousness establishes it as a feature of class politics that depends upon the elaboration of labor power's reflexive aspect, its status as the society of the producers, and therefore as an historically universal principle of community. It suggests that the society of producers is, in part, a way of generating discourses about a shared condition and the history in which it is shared; which is to say that it incorporates a principle of collective learning from the collectivist experience of capitalist production. It is in this regard that Marxian political sociology can be said to require a sociology of communication that is also a sociology of community (cf. Habermas 1979; Williams 1980).

POLITICAL MOBILIZATION

This characterization of class consciousness provides some understanding of the process of political mobilization (cf. Brown and Goldin 1973). The issue is not simply whether or not the establishment of organization and discipline among politically mobilized workers undermines the relevance of politics to experience (cf. Piven and Cloward 1982; Aronowitz 1973). It is rather the relationship between organizations and their universalizable content. This relationship, never fully secured, occurs only in the practical transformation of organization— in regard to the changing conditions of class struggle, within the expansion of capital, and in regard to opportunities already achieved.

It would be altogether romantic, ahistorical, and untheoretical to assume that the disposition to protest can be expressed only if organization and organizational authority stand aside.[2] First, protest does not reflect "disposition" in the sense of an impulse prior to the articulation of its conditions. Second, it is what it is as historically manifested and not as unmanifested potential. Third, it is a reification of organization to see it as an addition to rather than an intrinsic feature of politics, part of the dialectic of struggle (cf. Gramsci 1957). The internal critique of organization is also part of that dialectic but when that is converted into an external critique intolerant of its object, the scholar-critic becomes an outsider to practice and its conditions and hence at best irrelevant or at worst a source of practical divisiveness. But this has its own tragic inevitability where theory and practice are, as they must be, somewhat divided; and so the relationship between intellectuals and movements, too, is a dialectical one.

This in turn raises a sociological problem for labor: a social movement whose resources are never as great as its opponent's and whose practical composition is mixed and unevenly developed across politically limiting boundaries, is in constant danger—of dissolution, unpredictable reformation, and potentially catastrophic change. Its development is inevitably slow and problematic: it has its moments of democracy and its moments of discipline, its strategic successes and tactical failures. To judge it by taking a cross section of the course of its activity, to denounce it totally and undialectically at the points even of its least democratic formation, most obvious tactical breakdown, or simplest ideological expression, is itself uncritical, *"avant gardiste,"* hostile to the ideas of history and practice, and as much an instance of its own failure as the aspects of the movement it holds to judgement. To impose a utopian standard—of liberation, communism, or revolution—upon a social movement is to stand outside of history, to assume a position as indefensible epistemologically as it is practically (cf. Anderson 1976; Hobsbawm 1973; Anderson 1980). Regardless of their philosophical "bad faith," such judgments are part of labor's historic predicament, an understandable division of subjectivity, given the conditions of labor's political development, and an unavoidable feature of the inevitably unsteady relationship between left politics and left intellectual work.

The sociology of political mobilization must deal with its development through momentary conjunctures as well as its historical conditions: the imbeddedness of class-based movements in the contexts that operate at any moment of capitalist development. It must deal with political organization as a thorny feature of mobilization and as an aspect of the dialectic of reconciliation that moves in regard to class interest, local manifestations of capitalist production, political practices already in motion, the unevenness of any political development in the context of the uneven development of capital, the inevitable lag between labor's development and capital's, and the vicissitudes of power, force, and violence that class relations impose on politics. To judge labor by its appearance at a moment is to treat whatever practical compromise is reached in this dialectic of reconciliation as if it were a permanent state or the reflection of a fixed disposition. It is as if personality were to be described in purely dispositional terms and as a permanent structure of traits rather than, as Freud insisted, in terms of momentary compromises within the dialectic of impulse and control; or as if one were to evaluate a revolution by its immediate accomplishments, its post-revolutionary moment of structure, or by its failure to establish on schedule the utopia it had proclaimed to be its goal.

The tendency to judge is one of the marks of the problematic relationship between intellectuals and the movements they serve, between extra-practical theory and extra-theoretical practice. But it, too, must not be judged—as if the real work is practice and intellectual work is somehow false or irrelevant. Both are part of a dialectic; and their reconciliation, like the history of reconciling different aspects of labor's struggle, is a process fraught as always with difficulties, shifts and turns, temptations, disappointments, and impatience.

False Consciousness

The historical dimension of class consciousness has a negative as well as positive form. The positive form involves, as stated above, "the incorporation in action of the separation of and relation between purpose and activity." What is progressive in class consciousness is "the incorporation in action," the assignment of the contradiction to a process of development or learning through the practical acknowledgment of reason, organization, power, uneven development, and the rest.

There is, however, an antihistorical, regressive form as well, a temptation to consciousness and organization that represents the possible failure of that history in regard to which society can be realized. The overwhelming index of this potential negativity is repetition implemented, as it must be, by a discipline that feeds on itself more than on its historical conditions. It can be studied in terms of the concepts of "trait" and "structure" only on condition that the abstractly fixed character suggested by these concepts is finally understood in terms of its mediations, the pressures that sustain that character against the positive restoration of the dialectical movement toward society's realization.

The psychology of dispositional traits has catalogued a variety of regressive forms of consciousness, patterns marked only by the extremely mediated impulse to repetition. Marxian social psychologists have used the term "false consciousness" to refer to the same thing, though more for reasons of practice than to develop a model of permanent orientations. Their problem has been to explain how an essentially historical process comes to be blocked, or transformed into something hostile to the process of realizing society. In other words, the problem has been to provide a model or abstraction of the possible loss of historicity in order to suggest ways in which an intervention might produce a more extended historical reflection than is otherwise possible in the midst of history.

The appearance of the term "consciousness" in the phrase "false consciousness" tends to work the same mischief it works in "class consciousness." "False consciousness" is often used uncritically to indicate the failure of a particular group or population to achieve a "theoretically adequate" discourse on the capitalist mode of production (cf. Gabel, 1975; Lukacs, 1971). This particularly extreme segregation of theory and practice may be helpful for the critique of political strategies for class-based organizations, but it is not as such part of Marxian theory and in fact may disguise a decidedly nonhistorical politics of therapy, education, or guidance by a properly theoretically tutored elite (cf. Habermas 1973).

For class consciousness to be considered "false," in order to demonstrate by abstraction its potentially regressive and repetitive aspects, more is needed than the criticism of political discourses on the grounds that they are adequate only if theory is arbitrarily separated from practice. It is necessary first to show the forms of repetition and regression that are possible within the contradiction of capital and society and then to describe them abstractly in order to show how that relationship might work and how it might appear in experience. Such an analysis begins by recognizing the various temptations inherent in any political movement, negative though some of those might be. This is the only way in which the study of consciousness remains consistent with the contradictory character of capitalist development and therefore adequate to the history of class struggle.

Harold Garfinkel's "ethnomethodology," Freudian psychoanalysis, and literary theory are the most important theoretical resources presently available for clarifying the concept (cf. Eagleton 1983, for an account of contemporary theories of literature).

Freud argued that the antihistorical tendency, an uncritical and therefore sterilizing attitude toward the self, arises as a defense against the expression of needs whose means of gratification belong to indescribably punitive figures of power (for example, the father). To admit such needs to awareness is to risk their expression and consequently pain beyond calculation. To ensure against such an admission requires a denial of any historical dynamic whatsoever in the self—a denial that there are needs that cannot be restricted and that there are restrictions that cannot be tolerated. At the same time, the very act of denial becomes a basis for new needs that cannot be restricted, that are relatively autonomous of the conditions that give rise to them, and that constitute sources of new types of gratification. The antihistorical perspective, understandable within the dialectic of self-development, is thereby shown to feed on itself and to become its own desire. Similarly, the denial of one's own vulnerability to change must imply a denial of others. Two results follow: on the one hand ceaseless distraction and a corresponding absorption of self in an authority whose will is external to that self and therefore whose dictates seem impossible to restrict; and on the other an intolerance of those who point to or remind the self of its own inescapable contradictory condition and historicity (cf. above).

Freud's point was not that this is a pathological formation, but that it is an aspect of the normal development of the personality, a possibility inherent in the contradiction of impulse and control. Some writers have argued that this "natural" resistance to self-knowledge and the intolerance of the critical acts of others take an extreme and relatively fixed form under capitalism (Fromm 1955; Schneider 1975). As such, they become the foundation of a false consciousness that manifests itself either as apathy, subservient gratitude, or aggressive authoritarianism—the attitude of one who knows his or her substantiality only through the "master's" project. In any case, false consciousness is represented as a highly generalized attitude manifest primarily in the context of conventional politics, usually as fascist or liberal extremes neutralized by a mass culture. Above all, however, it is not considered part of the history of consciousness so much as it is an externally induced pathology that can only be corrected therapeutically, outside of collective practice, or through the intervention of some extra-political agency that is somehow above political reproach—intellectual elites, vanguard parties, and so on (cf. Habermas 1973).

This approach to false consciousness reminds us of the value of psychoanalysis for conceptualizing the historical dimension of personality consistent with Marxian metatheory. But it risks re-inserting a psychology of individuals into an essentially sociological inquiry that had, in regard to the historical critique of capital, rejected it in principle. Apathy and authoritarianism are undoubtedly likely in momentarily failed politics—witness the present situation in the United States—where political participation has little obvious connection with the facts of power and the purposes of policy. But they need not be uniquely characteristic of capitalism or characteristic of capitalism in all its phases.

False consciousness, in the sense of the negative side of class consciousness, as a temptation inherent in class struggle, cannot be conceived of as an attribute of individuals but only as an analytic feature of class. The problem is not so much to explain the empirical conditions of its appearance, growth, dissolution, or practical realization, but to apply a Marxian theory that includes false consciousness as a feature of analysis to all phenomena connected with capitalism. The concept serves to remind us, from that point of view, of the uneven development of labor's struggle within the uneven development of capitalism itself.

Harold Garfinkel's ethnomethodology consists of procedures for describing human conduct as the reflexive practices of collectivities (cf. Garfinkel 1967; Heritage 1984). This refers to that aspect of activity that confirms, or reproduces, or "accomplishes" the formal conditions under which each bit of activity displays its connection with, account-ability to, everything else that is being done—that is, displays its character as part of something greater than itself. Those formal condi-tions are said in turn to constitute a "setting" that transforms mere participation into complicit membership and participants into "mem-bers to a setting."[3]

The most general analytic principle of ethnomethodology is that every meaningful gesture, everything that can be called part of action, is simultaneously a relation of subject to object and subjectivity to self. But since the meaning of any gesture is established collectively as a matter of practice, the subject that is the issue in these relations is not an individual person but the whole process of intentionality that characterizes a given collectivity in a given set of circumstances. Thus, every social act reconstitutes the collective base of its responsiveness to the world.

The analytic principle can be restated more precisely: every gesture is shown to have been significant when it is described as both a relation of collectivity to a momentarily individualized object (the object of a concrete act, its focus or referent) and a relation of collectivity (virtu-ally realized as a practice) to the development of collectivity as condition of any further activity. Everything that an "individual" does is therefore initially merely a bit of activity awaiting the significance that its socialization will accomplish. It is part of the history of the setting that on its own account provides conditions for and the sense of action. For Garfinkel, motivations, commitments, and reasons are features of collective experience, part of the "on-going accomplish-ment" involved in realizing collectivity through collective practice. It follows as well that reflective and critical processes originate in settings and not in individuals taken abstractly from their settings.[4]

Ethnomethodology is the most rigorous and promising conceptuali-zation of consciousness as subjectivity that is consistent with the epistemological requirements of Marxian theory and that avoids a reduction of subjectivity to the psychology of individual persons. Like psychoanalysis, it comprehends human affairs historically. Because it does not rest with the abstraction of individuals and the corresponding abstraction of "object relations" (as in theories of perception, motiva-tion, and learning) it is a fuller realization of the project of showing how everything people do is part of their social development (and part of their contribution to sociality) before it can be a feature of their individual development in any sense whatsoever. Ethnomethodology is essentially the sociology of praxis, a study of how people acknowledge in their joint activities those conditions of action that they have collectively produced in such a way that the acknowledgement is a feature of reflection and part of an internal critique.[5]

It would be worthwhile for the sociology of capitalism to explore further the significance of ethnomethodology for Marxism (cf. Brown 1979b). At this point, however, a more modest discussion is sufficient to indicate its contribution to the analysis of the positive aspect of false consciousness. From this point of view, Garfinkel's research can be seen as similar to that of the structuralists: to describe human activity in such a way that it is impossible to impute to the parties, "members to a setting," an interest in "why we are not doing other than what we are doing." The difference between Garfinkel's work and that of many structuralists is the emphasis on self-critical process—on-going accomplishment—and the insistence that interaction be analyzed as a production in which the creation of sensible interactions is a strictly non-reiterative "ongoing accomplishment" against possible, tempting alternatives. Garfinkel goes beyond the structuralist idealization of the most extreme form false consciousness can take, and shows how the members' apparent "disinterest" in reflection is an active one and a feature of a progressive movement that must ultimately confront its own "external" mediations (cf. Goffman 1961b for a clear statement of the same phenomenon).

While the methodology is complex and difficult to describe without examples, it is possible to give some sense of it by mentioning several of its features. First, Garfinkel studies unplanned discourse, "conversation" treated as an "uninterrupted" series of meaning-pregnant but not meaning-realized gestural exchanges. The fact that the data used in conversational analysis show a great deal of interruption (silences, laughter, and so on), allows analysis to highlight, against the model of continuous circulation, collective actions aimed at obliterating, transforming, or modifying the effects of interruption (cf. Sacks 1974). These are then considered to be instances of the *work* members do to recover the sense of continuity necessary for reliable collective process. Since that recovery cannot be complete, its prospect requires a continuation of work as production, the primary (and contradictory) mechanism recognized by ethnomethodologists as base for the realization of sociality.

Typical characterizations of conversation refer to the historical character of its work—the facts that 1. it is intrinsically problematic for its parties, 2. it is an unrepeatable yet ordered series of activities, and 3. each moment of the series cannot be fully understood from outside it. The third implies that no moment can be remembered sensibly or even recorded without imputing (from an altogether external position) a quasi-structured and historical background to the conversational activity as a whole; and this requires imputing to it other items not articulated but apparently implicit in it. That is, the study of conversation as well as its own memory requires inventive reconstruction that in turn poses conflicts among the various practices that could be claimed to be valid reconstructions (cf. Brown 1983-84). This implies that the self reflective aspect (internal or external) of settings is the aspect of an internal dynamic similar to the conflict of interests discussed earlier.

The unit of analysis suggested by this characterization consists of a subseries of gestures that the observer has some reason to, but parties cannot take as, a completed text or set. While each element of the subseries is at least partly performed by an individual person, its sense depends upon the text, or set, performed collectively; and its recognizability as collective performance depends in part upon characterizing what the individual does as a display of what it is to be a "member to" this rather than "to" an alternative setting. Since any speaker's commitment to what she or he is saying depends upon the possibility that it will make intimate sense, individuals are understood in their relationship to the collectivity on which that production depends and against other such possible relationships. What they say, no less than how they speak, displays the exclusivity of their membership to the setting in relation to which "interruption" can be identified and the work of reproducing what is interrupted undertaken.

These members, these parties to conversation, work together in media. The paradigmatic medium for the ethnomethodologists is discursive language, which is why their procedures resemble what in literary study is called poetics (cf. White 1973). Given the emphasis on discourse, the collective product of a conversational process is not to be found within or in regard to the ostensible topic of the interaction but in the history of the setting itself. Conversation is, in its most essential quality, about itself. That is to say that it is about the possibility of further conversation among these particular socialized parties, or parties who can display membership and in so doing transform its conditions. By speaking together in the way that they do and with the materials that are at hand, they produce the possibility of continuing to speak together.

Garfinkel points out that individual speakers cannot be the subjects or controlling agents of the history of their conversation because they cannot, in principle, either intend and cognize it as a whole or even intend that their spoken moments make a difference to it as a whole. They are tied to the "objective" function of speaking: they can only speak about things if their speech is to be in the "ordinary course" of a conversation (cf. Schutz 1970).

Speech about things depends upon the social relations of speaking and must contribute to them or speech would soon end. The analytically real subject of the history of a conversation is, then, the collectivity that learns by means of the acts of its parties, and that is the setting to which every individual act is either radically appropriate or radically outside altogether. Conversation can be said to be social relations learning about themselves and, in that learning, transforming the conditions of their future. Individual acts of speech are instances of that learning and not something observable and describable outside of that history.

Garfinkel recognizes both an abstract and a concrete aspect of conversation, and a local and supra-local aspect of the discursive medium. The concrete element is the individualized gesture. This has a form and an objective content. But it is distinct only at the abstracted moment of its utterance. This moment is part of analysis. It serves merely as a limit for the observer, indicating no more than the minimal conditions of speech "recognizably being done," establishing an analytically minimal speaker. This minimal speaker is, for ethnomethodology, the observer's principle of the possibility that what is said can be understood out of context, one might say "as surreal" relative to the conversation as real subject. This is essential since ethnomethodological research begins by noting the fact that a given statement by itself (placed arbitrarily in another context than that of its use) cannot be interpreted as intra-conversational, or must be seen in any case as "odd." *Noting the possible oddness of an utterance is the first methodological condition of noticing its setting and ascribing to that setting a certain historicity.*

Given the concrete moment of conversation, Garfinkel concentrates on the abstract aspect of every gesture—not its momentary objective content or its temporary form as an utterance, but what it has in common with every other gesture—that is, the fact that it is produced collectively as the result of the labor of an ensemble. However, while the production of each gesture is collective, and while it is put into circulation in relation with all the other gestures that are at hand (the gesture, like labor power, is borne to the situation of meaning-constituting exchange), its actual appropriation to its setting occurs only in the "return" of the minimal speaker, the display of sense that occurs when a next speaker chooses to interpret an utterance as an instance of the normal against the odd usage. The point is that a conversation comes to be filled with gestures some of which guarantee, against possible interruption, that any subsequent one will be capable of circulating (entering the medium of collective realization).

Several problematic aspects of interaction are brought to notice in this: first the unrepeatability of a conversational series ensures that a great deal of what would be essential for a perfect appropriation of meaning will be missing at any given moment. This gives the concrete act of speaking its contradictory relation to the abstract property of what is spoken: we (as parties to "conversation") never say what is meant nor mean what is said. Second, for something to make sense it must contribute not simply to a static structure but to a history, to the progress of conversational productivity. It must not only circulate, it must be made appropriate to a further circulation that includes its own appearance as an item in the series: it must not only circulate, it must be used in the sense of being withdrawn from circulation.

A conversation in which one party arrogates an authority foreign to the democratic principle of conversation, in which an individual or individuals attempt to manage the utterances or name the discourse of the parties, will exhibit the self-defeating aspect of production typical of any situation that depends upon social production but is organized and stratified in the interest of private parties. Garfinkel idealizes conversation as an authentic, socially progressive form. This clarifies the possibility of continuity but begs some crucial questions about direction. It assumes as part of its analysis that the circulation of gestures is compatible with their use (extraction from circulation) in the furtherance of that circulation. But even with that assumption, it is clear that there must be some contradiction of circulation and use, if only because there must be the moment of choice, a minimal speaker. And the principle of that moment of choice allows for the possible selection of an utterance for which no appropriation is possible—a deviation from sense and recognizable productivity (cf. Sacks 1974).

Third, the fact that the medium of conversation is discursive language suggests that there is something on the order of a message unit, something that is distinct for an observer as well as the parties, that comprises an utterance. There are, Garfinkel notes, two bases for interpreting such units: one is in terms of the particular history that is this, that, or the other conversation; the other is in terms of a wider setting, something like conversation but more inclusive and less intimate. In the first, meanings indicate the concreteness of the setting, the locale; in the second, meanings indicate an idealized universe of discourse without ambiguities, a societal store of sense and sensibility, a utopia of "ordinary language."

Whenever we speak, we are speaking *to* another or others, but *for* the most general of possible audiences. The intimate interpersonal aspect of communication is intersected by the wider universe of putatively shared meanings—in principle but not in actual practice since that wider universe is merely the other limit to the minimal speaker, the point at which speech turns against its own possibility by undermining its setting in favor of the speaker's interest in other inescapable settings. Every act of speech is a reconciliation of the actor with his or her setting, and a reconciliation of two appropriations of the act: to the particular setting and to the most general social conditions possible beyond the particular setting. These reconciliations, however, are project rather than possibility, promise rather than possible accomplishment, and therefore are dynamic and historical aspects of conversation, not structures or rules.

But Garfinkel's is still the picture of a history that cannot sustain itself as history. In order for the parties to convey an awareness, a sense, of their conversation as such, in order for the production of meaning to comprehend and reflect upon its own process, to become intellectual, critical, and activist about itself, there must be something external to and presupposed by the setting. Whatever this might be, it must answer the question: under what circumstances do individuals ask, and not ask, "why aren't we doing other than what we are doing?" Obviously, part of the answer comes from ethnomethodology itself, its employment of procedures that show how acts must depend upon inherently ambiguous conditions that are produced but cannot be a topic or object.

The idea of intimacy implicit in this account of the use of language in discourse is itself in need of explanation, as Garfinkel has recognized in his demand for an ethnomethodology of ethnomethodology. We have indicated one possible line of explanation in our discussion of Goffman's work. Whether or not this is adequate to expand the historical dynamic implicit in ethnomethodological research cannot be decided here. What is important is the connection between Garfinkel's account and the concept of false consciousness.

The very restriction of his notion of conversation to activities of particular parties operating within a specific boundary with determinate materials shows the incompleteness of his identification of the phenomenon, though there is a suggestion of the expanded notion in the relation between speaking and using meanings established beyond the context of speaking. His is, regardless, an adequate abstraction of consciousness from the practice side of the theory-practice relationship implicit in Marxian epistemology.

Garfinkel constructs realistic situations that are on the order of independent life cycles. His accounts of interactions as insular but troubled are dramatically credible as well as dialectical. They are situations in regard to which the reader/observer knows the observed parties as acting in such a way that the question "why aren't we doing other than what we are doing?" does not arise, and yet such that their interposition is not a fixed structure or disposition. To the extent that he does this, he raises the question of critique, possible intervention, mediation, and politics.

But this brings us back to the world of capitalist production, its uneven development, contradictions and paradoxes, and its sociological ramifications. It is there that class consciousness finds its mediations and, in turn, displays itself as part of the history of capitalism. And it should be clear that that history is not the history of this or that nation but the dynamic of a certain form of modernism, a world in which capital's expansion has become global, the class struggle superimposed upon geopolitical divisions inherited from ages of empire but recast as divisions within a world economy, and the national, social, political, and cultural forms that had been taken for granted as part of democracy, progress, modernization, and the rest, systematically challenged by previous unimagined concentrations of wealth and mobilizations of peoples (cf. Amin 1976; Wallerstein 1974).

> The need of a constantly expanding market for its products chases the bourgeoisie over the whole surface of the globe. It must nestle everywhere, settle everywhere, establish connections everywhere.
> The bourgeoisie has through its exploitation of the world market given a cosmopolitan character to the great chagrin of reactionaries, it has drawn from under the feet of industry the national ground on which it stood. [Marx and Engels 1948]

Notes

1. One bears labor power as one bears a burden, sells in a desperation of need, and subjects oneself to the will of another in an attitude of being possessed and awaiting replacement.

2. This is one assumption of present-day criticisms of parties and unions that has arisen in the context of the various movements that have made the past decades so volatile and promising to the prospects of humanist ideals. But criticism goes too far when it fails to recognize the practical universalization posed by class movements and begs the question of their integration with other movements by denying the power-organizational dimension of politics and the historical limits of any movement's development under capitalism.

3. For example, asking a question idly, without intending to request a response (as in "I wonder if it will rain today") may nevertheless be followed by one. If so, the response may mark itself as a response rather than another idle speech gesture by its pacing, attack, or release. Thus, "I don't really care" may demand a further reply, and therefore be part of the accomplishment of a setting, if there is a provocative emphasis on any one of the words; if the last word is held long enough to indicate that caring about weather is on a list of priorities, but low on the list, and therefore suggesting a possible interaction about caring in general; if pauses occur between the words that indicate an inviting pregnancy in what is being said or an attitude of waiting on the part of the speaker; etc.

4. Garfinkel, unlike Goffman, has not developed the notion of "individual" beyond this, but it would appear that for him, as for Goffman, what we call "the individual" is the perpetrator of a bit of activity to which responsibiltiy for the whole act is assigned for reasons established collectively. This assumes a certain tension between the perpetrator as agent of the bit and the perpetrator as an instance of a competing process of socializing meaning (cf. Shutz 1967), an ambiguity that is at the heart of all activity and that reflects a more general alienation than that usually thought of as objectification.

5. Garfinkel explores the relation of internal critique to its setting in his undeveloped commentary on the nature of sociological reasoning—"members doing sociology." This is the area that needs further work if ethnomethodology is to realize its promise as a critical-historical discipline (cf. Heritage 1984).

11

Conclusion

Marxism is the critique of capitalism, the theory of the capitalist political economy from the standpoint of social labor. And since labor's relation to capital is one of class struggle, it expresses what has become relevant to and significant within that struggle. It is, essentially, that critique that points to the possible realization of society, and therefore to the possibility of sociology and its adjacent disciplines.

While Marxian sociology has a great deal to say about the traditional sociological topics, it has its own embracing subject matter. Daily life, class, exploitation, the accumulation of capital, resistance, and uneven development are areas of research in which Marxian theory is unsurpassed. It has, as well, its own methods and concepts derived from the meta-theoretical emphasis on history and sociality. Finally, it has its practical foundation in the interest in overcoming exploitation, the interest in cooperation and therefore society itself. Because of this and because it highlights the relation of wealth and power to the problematic of society, it remains the main source within the social sciences of an intellectual formulation of the ideals of democracy. Here, the uneven development of capitalism provides the clues, the critical analysis of capitalist wealth the solution.

The enormous number of contemporary Marxian journals and books published during the past decade testifies to the increasing importance of Marxian thought in American social science and literary studies. These are crucial resources for the continuing and expanded critique of capital; they are evidence as well of the relevance, creativity, vitality, and determination of Marxian scholars. They are part of what remains of one of our preeminent traditions of scholarship and political practice. Much of what is critical and/or novel in contemporary American sociology, historiography, and political science can be traced either to encounters with the Marxian literature, attempts to avoid it, or to its indirect influence. Since much that is theoretically interesting in American sociology at present (so far as the relationship between society and history is concerned) involves language studies and Marxism, it has been worthwhile exploring the possible connections between these two literatures as a basis for a Marxian sociology. The current conflict within the discipline remains that identified so long ago by C. Wright Mills: between the academic entrepreneurs ("professionals") who sell their services to business and the state (cf. Lazarsfled et al. 1967a), and those who insist, still against odds, that sociology is a discipline constituting adjacent disciplines, a critical practice, a reflection upon the relationship between society and history, and part of the prospect for a realization of the society as yet only promised.

When people speak of ideas that revolutionize society, they do but express the fact, that within the old society, the elements of a new one have been created, and that the dissolution of the old ideas keeps even pace with the dissolution of the old conditions of existence. [Marx and Engels, *The Communist Manifesto,* 1948]

In the social production which men carry on they enter into definite relations that are indispensable and independent of their will; these relations of production correspond to a definite stage of development of their material powers of production. The sum total of these relations of production constitutes the economic structure of society—the real foundation, on which rise legal and political superstructures and to which correspond definite forms of social consciousness. The mode of production in material life determines the general characters of the social, political, and spiritual processes of life. It is not the consciousness of men that determines their existence, but, on the contrary, their social existence determines their consciousness. At a certain stage of their development the material forces of production in society come into conflict with the existing relations of production, or—what is but a legal expression for the same thing—with the property relations within which they had been at work before. From forms of development of the forces of production these relations turn into their fetters. Then comes the period of social revolution. With the changes of the economic foundation the entire immense superstructure is more or less rapidly transformed. [Marx, *A Contribution to the Critique of Political Economy,* 1970]

Bibliography

Adorno, T. 1976. "Introduction." In T. Adorno, H. Albert, R. Dahrendorf, J. Habermas, H. Pilot, and K. Popper, *The Positivist Dispute in German Sociology.* New York: Harper & Row. 1–67.

Adorno, T., E. Frenkel-Brunswik, D. Levinson, and R. Sanford. 1950. *The Authoritarian Personality.* New York: Harper & Row.

Aglietta, M. 1979. *A Theory of Capitalist Regulation: The U.S. Experience.* London: New Left Books.

Althusser, L. 1970. *For Marx.* New York: Vintage.

———. 1971. *Lenin and Philosophy.* New York: Monthly Review Press.

Amin, S. 1976. *Unequal Development: An Essay on the Social Formation of Peripheral Capitalism.* New York: Monthly Review Press.

Amin, S., A. Giovanni, A. G. Frank, I. Wallerstein. 1982. *Dynamics of Global Crisis.* New York: Monthly Review Press.

Anderson, P. 1976. *Considerations on Western Marxism.* London: New Left Books.

———. 1983. *Arguments Within English Marxism.* London: Verso.

Arato, A., and E. Gebhardt, eds. 1978. *The Essential Frankfurt School Reader.* New York: Urizen Books.

Aronowitz, S. 1973. *False Promises.* New York: McGraw-Hill.

———. 1981. *The Crisis in Historical Materialism.* New York: Praeger.

———. 1983. *Working Class Hero: A New Strategy for Labor.* New York: Pilgrim Press.

Avineri, S. 1968. *The Social and Political Thought of Karl Marx.* Cambridge: Cambridge University Press.

Bakhtin, M. 1968. *Rabelais and His World.* Translated by H. Iswolsky. Cambridge: MIT Press.

———. 1981. *The Dialogic Imagination.* Translated by C. Emerson and M. Holquist; edited by M. Holquist. Austin: University of Texas Press.

Barthes, R. 1972. *Mythologies.* New York: Hill & Wang.

———. 1977. *Image-Music-Text.* Translated by S. Heath. New York: Hill & Wang.

Bell, D. 1976. *The Cultural Contradictions of Capitalism.* New York: Harper & Row.

Bittner, E. 1965. "The Concept of Organization." *Social Research* 32: 230–255.

Blackburn, R., ed. 1978. *Revolution and Class Struggle*. Atlantic Highlands: Humanities Press.

Blau, P., and M. Meyer. 1971. *Bureaucracy in Modern Society,* 2nd ed. New York: Random House.

Block, F. 1977. *The Origins of International Economic Disorder*. Berkeley: University of California Press.

Blum, A., and P. McHugh. 1984. *Self Reflection in the Arts and Sciences*. Atlantic Highlands: Humanities Press.

Bottomore, T. 1975. *Marxist Sociology*. London: Macmillan.

Bottomore, T., L. Harris, V. Kiernan, R. Miliband, eds. 1983. *A Dictionary of Marxist Thought*. Cambridge: Harvard University Press.

Bowles, S., and H. Gintis. 1976. *Schooling in Capitalist America*. New York: Basic Books.

Braverman, H. 1975. *Labor and Monopoly Capital*. New York: Monthly Review Press.

Brown, M. "Ethnomethodology as Dialectical Reason." Paper presented at meeting of The American Sociological Association, 1977.

———. 1978. "The New City and the Myth of the Primary." *Journal of Comparative Urban Research:* 54–69.

———. 1979a. "Society Against the State: The Fullness of the Primitive." *October* 6: 61–73.

———. 1979b. "Sociology as Critical Theory." *Theoretical Perspectives in Sociology,* edited by S. McNall. New York: St. Martin's Press.

———. 1983–84. "Ideology and the Metaphysics of Content." *Social Text* 8: 55–83.

Brown, M., and A. Goldin. 1973. *Collective Behavior*. Pacific Palisades, Ca.: Goodyear.

Burawoy, M. 1979a. "Contemporary Currents in Marxist Theory." *Theoretical Perspectives in Sociology,* edited by S. McNall. New York: St. Martin's Press.

———. 1979b. *Manufacturing Consent*. Chicago: Chicago University Press.

Burke, P. 1978. *Popular Culture in Early Modern Europe*. London: Temple Smith.

———. 1980. *Sociology and History*. London: Allen & Unwin.

Chomsky, N., and E. Herman. 1979. *The Washington Connection and Third World Fascism*. Boston: South End Press.

Cicourel, A. 1964. *Method and Measurement in Sociology*. London: Collier-Macmillan.

———. 1974. *Cognitive Sociology*. New York: Free Press.

Clarke, S. 1982. *Marx, Marginalism and Modern Sociology*. London: Macmillan.

Clastres, P. 1977. *Society Against the State*. Translated by Robert Hurley and Abe Stein. New York: Urizen Books.

Clawson, D. 1980. *Bureaucracy and the Labor Process*. New York: Monthly Review Press.

Cohen, G. A. 1979. *Karl Marx's Theory of History: A Defence*. Oxford: Oxford University Press.

Cohen, J., and J. Rogers. 1983. *On Democracy*. Middlesex: Penguin.

Dahlgren, P. "Network TV News and the Corporate State." Ph.D. diss., City University of New York, 1977.

Davis, M. 1980a. "The Barren Marriage of American Labour and the Democratic Party." *New Left Review* 124 (Nov.–Dec.)

———. 1980b. "Why the U.S. Working Class is Different." *New Left Review* 123: (Sept.-Oct.).

Deleuze, G., and F. Guattari. 1977. *Anti-Oedipus*. New York: Viking.

Domhoff, W. 1967. *Who Rules America*. Englewood Cliffs: Prentice-Hall.

———. 1980. *Power Structure Research*. Beverly Hills: Sage Publications.

Dumont, L. 1977. *From Mandeville to Marx*. Chicago: University of Chicago Press.

Eagleton, T. 1983. *Literary Theory*. Minneapolis: University of Minnesota Press.

Ecker, M. "Labor and the State: Productivity as a Social Process." Ph.D. diss., City University of New York, 1983.

Edwards, R. 1979. *Contested Terrain: The Transformation of the Workplace in the Twentieth Century*. New York: Basic Books.

Elster, J. 1985. *Making Sense of Marx*. New York: Cambridge University Press.

Engels, F. 1973. *The Condition of the Working Class in England*. Moscow: Progress.

Etzioni, A. 1968. *The Active Society*. Glencoe, Ill.: Free Press.

Ewen, S. 1976. *Captains of Consciousness*. New York: McGraw-Hill.

Flacks, R., and G. Turkel. 1978. "Radical Sociology: The Emergence of NeoMarxian Perspectives in U.S. Sociology." *Annual Review of Sociology* 4: 193–238.

Foner, P. 1972. *History of the Labor Movement in the United States*. 5 vols. New York: International.

Foucault, M. 1973a. *The Birth of the Clinic*. New York: Vintage.

———. 1973b. *The Order of Things*. New York: Pantheon.

———. 1977. *Discipline and Punish*. New York: Random House.

———. 1980. *The History of Sexuality*. Vol. 1, New York: Vintage.

Fromm, E. 1955. *The Sane Society*. New York: Rinehart.

Gabel, J. 1975. *False Consciousness*. London: Blackwells.

Garfinkel, H. 1967. *Studies in Ethnomethodology*. Englewood Cliffs: Prentice-Hall.

Giddens, A. 1980. *A Contemporary Critique of Historical Materialism.* Berkeley: University of California Press.

———. 1982. *Sociology: A Brief But Critical Introduction.* New York: Harcourt Brace Jovanovitch Inc.

Gitlin, T. 1980. *The Whole World is Watching.* Berkeley: University of California Press.

Gleicher, D. 1985–1986. "The Ontology of Labor Values: Remarks on the *Science & Society* Value Symposium." *Science & Society,* XLIX, Number 4: 463–471 (Winter).

Goffman, E. 1959. *The Presentation of Self in Everyday Life.* New York: Doubleday.

———. 1961a. *Asylums.* New York: Anchor Books.

———. 1961b. *Encounters.* New York: Bobbs-Merrill.

———. 1963. *Stigma.* Englewood Cliffs: Prentice-Hall.

———. 1974. *Frame Analysis: An Essay on the Organization of Experience.* New York: Harper & Row.

Gordon, D., R. Edwards, and M. Reich. 1982a. *Segmented Work, Divided Workers: The Historical Transformation of Labor in the United States.* New York: Cambridge University Press.

Gordon, D., and the staff of the Institute for Labor Education and Research. 1982b. *What's Wrong With the U.S. Economy: A Popular Guide for the Rest of Us.* Boston: South End Press.

Gorz, A. 1967. *Strategy for Labor.* Boston: Beacon Press.

———. 1976. *The Division of Labor.* Atlantic Highlands, New Jersey: Humanities Press.

Gouldner, A. 1970. *The Coming Crisis of Western Sociology.* New York: Basic Books.

———.1976. *The Dialectic of Ideology and Technology.* New York: Seabury.

———. 1982. *Two Marxisms.* New York: Oxford University Press.

Gramsci, A. 1957. *The Modern Prince and Other Writings.* London: Lawrence & Wishart.

Gross, B. 1980. *Friendly Fascism: The New Face of Power in America.* New York: M. Evans.

Gurr, T. 1969. "A Comparative Study of Civil Strife." In *Violence in America: A Report to the National Commission on the Causes and Prevention of Violence, June 1969.* edited by H. Graham and T. Gurr. New York: Signet.

Gutman, H. 1976. *Work, Culture, and Society in Industrializing America.* New York: Knopf.

Habermas, J. 1970a. "Technology and Science as 'Ideology.' " In J. Habermas, *Toward a Rational Society.* Boston: Beacon Press.

———. 1970b. "Toward a Theory of Communicative Competence." In *Recent Sociology,* edited by H. Dreitzel, vol. 2, 114–150. New York: Macmillan.

———. 1970c. *Toward a Rational Society.* Boston: Beacon Press.

———. 1971. *Knowledge and Human Interest.* Boston: Beacon Press.

———. 1973. *Theory and Practice*. Boston: Beacon Press.

———. 1975. *Legitimation Crisis*. Boston: Beacon Press.

Hall, S. 1977. "The 'Political' and the 'Economic' in Marx's Theory of Classes." In *Class and Class Structure*, edited by A. Hunt. London: Lawrence & Wishart.

Hammond, J. L., and B. Hammond. 1911. *The Village Labourer 1760–1832*. London.

Han, S. 1979. "Ideology—Critique and Social Science," in McNall. New York: St. Martin's Press.

Harvey, D. 1973. *Social Justice and the City*. Baltimore: Johns Hopkins Press.

Hay, D., et al. 1975. *Albion's Fatal Tree*. New York: Pantheon.

Hegel, G. W. 1967. *The Phenomenology of Mind*. New York: Harper & Row.

Heritage, J. 1984. *Garfinkel and Ethnomethodology*. Cambridge: Polity Press.

Hobsbawm, E. J. 1962. *The Age of Revolution*. London: Weidenfeld & Nicholson.

———. 1973. *Revolutionaries*. New York: New American Library.

———. 1981. *The Forward March of Labour Halted?* London: Verso.

Horkheimer, M., and T. Adorno. 1972. *Dialectic of Enlightenment*. New York: Seabury Press.

Howe, I. 1979. *Celebrations and Attacks: Thirty Years of Literary and Cultural Commentary*. New York: Horizon.

Jacoby, R. 1975. *Social Amnesia*. Boston: Beacon Press.

Jameson, F. 1971. *Marxism and Form*. Princeton: Princeton University Press.

———. 1981. *The Political Unconscious*. Ithaca: Cornell University Press.

———. 1984. "Periodizing the 60s." In *The 60s Without Apology*, edited by S. Sayres et al. Minneapolis: University of Minnesota Press.

Jay, M. 1973. *The Dialectical Imagination*. Boston: Little, Brown.

Jessop, B. 1982. *The Capitalist State*. New York: New York University Press.

Jones, G. S. 1971. *Outcast London*. Oxford: Oxford University Press.

Kesselman, M. 1982. "The State and Class Struggle: Trends in Marxist Political Science." In *The Left Academy*, vol. 1, edited by B. Ollman and E. Vernoff. New York: McGraw-Hill.

Kornblum, W. 1974. *Blue Collar Community*. Chicago: University of Chicago Press.

Kristeva, J. 1968. "La Sémiologie: Science critique et/ou critique de la science," *Tel Quel, theorie d'ensemble*. Paris: Editions du Seuil.

Laclau, E., and C. Mouffe. 1985. *Hegemony and Socialist Strategy*. Translated by W. Moore and P. Cammack. London: Verso.

Lasch, C. 1977. *Haven in a Heartless World*. New York: Basic Books.

Lazarsfeld, P., W. Sewell, and H. Wilensky, eds. 1967a. *The Uses of Sociology*. New York: Basic Books.

———. 1967b. "Introduction." In *The Uses of Sociology*. New York: Basic Books.

Lefebvre, H. 1971. *Everyday Life in the Modern World.* New York: Harper.

Levine, A. 1984. *Arguing for Socialism.* Boston: Routledge & Kegan Paul.

Lichten, E. "Class Struggle and Fiscal Crisis: New York City and the Development of Austerity." Ph.D. diss., City University of New York, 1981.

Lukacs, G. 1971. *History and Class Consciousness.* Cambridge: MIT Press.

Mandel, E. 1968. *Marxist Economic Theory.* 2 vols. New York: Monthly Review Press.

———. 1970. *An Introduction to Marxist Economic Theory.* New York: Pathfinder.

———. 1975. *Late Capitalism.* London: New Left Books.

———. 1980. *The Second Slump.* London: Verso.

March, J., and H. Simon. 1958. *Organizations.* New York: Wiley.

Marcuse, H. 1964. *One-Dimensional Man.* Boston: Beacon Press.

Martin, R. 1985. "Dance as a Social Movement." *Social Text* 12 (Fall).

Marx, K. 1967. *Capital.* Vol. 1. New York: International.

———. 1970. *A Contribution to the Critique of Political Economy.* New York: International.

———. 1973. *Grundrisse.* New York: Vintage.

———. 1976; 1981a; 1981b. *Capital.* 3 Volumes. Middlesex: Penguin.

———, and F. Engels, 1948. *The Communist Manifesto.* New York: International.

———, and F. Engels, 1970. *The German Ideology.* New York: International.

Mattelart, A. 1980. *Mass Media, Ideologies, and the Revolutionary Movement.* Atlantic Highlands, New Jersey: Humanities Press.

McClellan, D. 1977. *Karl Marx: His Life and Thought.* New York: Harper & Row.

———, ed. 1971. *The Thought of Karl Marx.* New York: Harper & Row.

McNall, S., ed. 1979. *Theoretical Perspectives in Sociology.* New York: St. Martin's Press.

Mepham, J., and D. Ruben, eds. 1979. *Issues in Marxist Philosophy.* 2 vols. Atlantic Highlands, New Jersey: Humanities Press.

Milgram, S. 1974. *Obedience to Authority.* New York: Harper & Row.

Miliband, R. 1969. *The State in Capitalist Society.* Oxford: Oxford University Press.

———. 1977. *Marxism and Politics.* Oxford: Oxford University Press.

Miliband, R., J. Saville, and M. Liebman, M., eds. 1984. *The Uses of Anti-Communism. Socialist Register, 1984.* London: Merlin Press.

Milkman, R. 1985. *Women, Work, and Protest: A Century of Women's Labor History.* Boston: Routledge & Kegan Paul.

Mills, C. W. 1956. *The Power Elite.* New York: Oxford University Press.

Moffit, M. 1983. *The World's Money.* New York: Simon & Schuster.

Montgomery, D. 1979. *Workers' Control in America*. New York: Cambridge University Press.

Neuberg, V. 1977. *Popular Literature*. Middlesex: Penguin.

O'Connor, J. 1973. *The Fiscal Crisis of the State*. New York: St. Martin's Press.

Offe, C. 1971. *Contradictions of the Welfare State*. Edited by J. Keane. Cambridge: Cambridge University Press.

Ollman, B. 1971. *Alienation—Marx's Conception of Man in Capitalist Society*. Cambridge: Cambridge University Press.

Ollman, B., and E. Vernoff, eds. 1982. *The Left Academy*. Vol. 1. New York: McGraw-Hill.

———. 1984. *The Left Academy*. Vol. 2. New York: Praeger.

Parsons, T. 1949. *The Structure of Social Action*. Glencoe, Ill.: Free Press.

———. 1951. *The Social System*. Glencoe, Ill.: Free Press.

Payer, C. 1982. *The World Bank: A Critical Analysis*. New York: Monthly Review Press.

Petras, J. 1985. "Authoritarianism, Democracy, and the Transition to Socialism." *Socialism and Democracy* 1 (Fall).

Piconne, P. 1975–76. "Review of Hugh Mehan and Houston Wood, *The Reality of Ethnomethodology*." *Telos* 26 (Winter).

Piven, F., and R. Cloward. 1982. *The New Class War*. New York: Pantheon.

Polanyi, K. 1944. *The Great Transformation*. Boston: Beacon Press.

Poster, M. 1978. *Critical Theory of the Family*. New York: Seabury Press.

Poulantzas, N. 1975a. *Classes in Contemporary Capitalism*. London: New Left Books.

———. 1975b. *Political Power and Social Classes*. London: New Left Books.

———. 1978. *State, Power, Socialism*. London: New Left Books.

Renner, K. 1949. *The Institutions of Private Law and Their Social Functions*. London: Routledge & Kegan Paul.

Resnick, S., and R. Wolff, eds. 1985. *Rethinking Marxism: Essays for Harry Magdoff and Paul Sweezy*. Brooklyn, N.Y.: Autonomedia.

Ricoeur, P. 1976. *Interpretation Theory*. Fort Worth: Texas Christian University Press.

Rogin, M. 1967. *The Intellectuals and McCarthy*. Cambridge: MIT Press.

Rubin, G. 1978. *Worlds of Pain: Life in the Working-Class Family*. New York: Basic Books.

Rudé, G. 1964. *The Crowd in History*. New York: Wiley.

———. 1980. *Ideology and Popular Protest*. New York: Pantheon.

Sacks, H. 1974. "An analysis of the course of a joke's telling in conversation." In *Explorations in the Ethnography of Speaking*, edited by R. Bauman and J. Sherzer. Cambridge: Cambridge University Press.

Said, E. 1977. "Zionism from the Standpoint of its Victims." "*Social Text* 1.

Samuel, R., ed. 1981. *People's History and Socialist Theory.* London: Routledge & Kegan Paul.

Sartre, J. 1963. *Search For a Method.* Translated by H. Barnes. New York: Random House.

———. 1964. *St. Genet.* New York: Mentor.

———. 1966. *What is Literature?* New York: Washington Square Press.

———. 1976. *Critique of Dialectical Reason.* London: New Left Books.

Schiller, H. 1971. *Mass Communications and American Empire.* Boston: Beacon Press.

Schneider, M. 1975. *Neurosis and Civilization: A Marxist/Freudian Synthesis.* Translated by M. Roloff. New York: Seabury Press.

Schroyer, T. 1973. *The Critique of Domination.* Boston: Beacon Press.

Schurmann, F. 1974. *The Logic of World Power.* New York: Pantheon.

Schutz, A. 1967. *The Phenomenology of the Social World.* Evanston, Ill.: Northwestern University Press.

———. 1970. *Reflections on the Problem of Relevance.* New Haven: Yale University Press.

Seashore, S. 1954. *Group Cohesiveness in the Industrial Work Group.* Ann Arbor: Survey Research Center, University of Michigan.

Sennett, R., and J. Cobb. 1972. *The Hidden Injuries of Class.* New York: Knopf.

Skocpol, T. 1979. *States and Revolutions.* New York: Cambridge University Press.

Small, A. 1972. *Adam Smith and Modern Sociology.* Clifton, New Jersey: A. M. Kelley. repr. of 1907 ed.

Smelser, N. 1963. *Theory of Collective Behavior.* New York: Free Press.

Sudnow, D. 1967. *Passing On.* Englewood Cliffs: Prentice-Hall.

Sweezy, P. 1968. *The Theory of Capitalist Development.* New York: Monthly Review Press.

Therborn, G. 1976. *Science, Class and Society: On the Formation of Sociology and Historical Materialism.* London: New Left Books.

Thompson, E. 1963. *The Making of the English Working Class.* New York: Knopf.

———. 1975. "The Crime of Anonymity." In *Albion's Fatal Tree,* edited by D. Hay, et al. New York: Pantheon.

———. 1978. *The Poverty of Theory.* New York: Monthly Review Press.

Tilly, C. 1978. *From Mobilization to Revolution.* Reading, Mass.: Addison-Wesley.

Turner, R. 1964. "Collective Behavior." In *Handbook of Modern Sociology,* edited by R. Faris. Chicago: Rand McNally.

Wallerstein, I. 1974. *The Modern World System.* New York: Academic Press.

———. 1983. *Historical Capitalism.* London: Verso.

White, H. 1973. *Metahistory.* Baltimore: Johns Hopkins University Press.

Williams, R. 1960. *Culture and Society*. New York: Doubleday.

———. 1961. *The Long Revolution*. London: Chatto & Windus.

———. 1975. *The Country and the City*. New York: Oxford University Press.

———. 1977. *Marxism and Literature*. Oxford: Oxford University Press.

———. 1980. *Problems in Materialism and Culture*. London: Verso.

Willis, P. 1977. *Learning to Labour*. Westmead: Saxon House.

Wolfe, A. 1973. *The Seamy Side of Democracy*. New York: David McKay.

———. 1977. *The Limits of Legitimacy*. New York: Free Press.

———. 1981. *America's Impasse: The Rise and Fall of the Politics of Growth*. Boston: South End Press.

Working Papers in Cultural Studies 10. 1977.

Wright, E. 1975. "Alternative Perspectives in the Marxist Theory of Accumulation and Crisis." *Insurgent Sociologist* 6, no. 1.

———. 1978. *Class, Crisis and the State*. London: New Left Books.

———. 1984. "A General Framework for the Analysis of Class Structure." *Politics & Society* 13, no. 4.

Zaretsky, E. 1976. *Capitalism, the Family, and Personal Life*. New York: Harper & Row.

Index